THE LIMITED KNOWLEDGE SERIES
VOLUME ONE

GOD'S MYSTERIES UNFOLDED ONE AFTER ANOTHER

By Pastor Obed Kirkpatrick

Copyright © 2006 by Pastor Obed Kirkpatrick

The Limited Knowledge Series Volume One
God's Mysteries Unfolded One After Another
by Pastor Obed Kirkpatrick

Printed in the United States of America

ISBN 1-59781-974-3

All rights reserved solely by the author. The author guarantees all contents are original and do not infringe upon the legal rights of any other person or work. No part of this book may be reproduced in any form without the permission of the author. The views expressed in this book are not necessarily those of the publisher.

Unless otherwise indicated, Bible quotations are taken from King James Bible.

www.xulonpress.com

Foreword
By Jerry Lockhart

Well over thirty years ago, Obed Kirkpatrick, chairman of the board of deacons at a large Alexandria, LA Baptist Church, was confronted with some Scripture which had never been brought to his attention. At first Bro. Kirkpatrick, not unlike most others, drew the too quick conclusion that it was being misinterpreted. After all, wasn't the historic tradition held by his church more valid than what some man said to him about these verses?!

Since it was his sister, Mrs. Bill (Susie) Burrell, who had confronted him and had brought in the "man" who showed these things to him, Bro. Obed decided he should help Susie and Bill get their doctrine straight. So he went to the Word of God and began to try to prove Bro. E. C. Moore wrong. Respect for the Book took him on a new and exciting journey through it in a way he had never come to see it before—dispensationally.

It turned out the things Bro. Moore was showing him were the truth. Bro. Obed had to come to grips with how the "doing" of churchy stuff had kept his knowledge limited. Things which the Lord wanted us to know and apply to us today had been put aside or on the way-back burner so that they didn't interfere with the current church emphasis. In his mind, then, things had to change. He began to show people. He began to understand that these things needed to be taught and preached. And before long Bro. Obed knew he needed to go preach it. So he did. He still does.

In the course of finding God's will in their life, The Kirkpatrick's moved to Baton Rouge and started a "grace" church. The five compiled doctrinal books which follow were written while he was Pastoring in Baton Rouge.

My first recollection of Bro. Obed was from a visit to Pineview Bible Camp in Alabama about 1975. Much water has run under the bridge since then and many souls have been saved by his preaching of the gospel of Christ as the power of God unto salvation. Bro. Obed and I have had many occasions for fellowship and for preaching on the same pulpit at conferences, camps, and *Academy of Bible Doctrine* classes. I praise the Lord for the privilege of this association.

As to these doctrines which he saw in the early '70s and which are presented here; they are very important because they show how the Apostle Paul not only received *first* the gospel of Christ—that Christ died for our sins, was buried, and was raised again for our justification—but that he also revealed in Scripture the great mysteries of God. How simple they are. How easily understood they are. How come churches and their ministers miss these great truths?

Many who would tell us they are Christians will reject these truths. Some for no more reason than that to receive these things, they would have to change...and they like themselves the way they are. Some for the simple reason that whatever they now believe was good enough for Daddy and Momma and it's good enough for them, too. Others might reject these truths because they have read the "church fathers" and have not found any revealed mysteries.

But you who might not fall into any of those categories, yet in some way reject true doctrine as you make the scriptural comparisons; let me say to you, "try the words: compare scripture with scripture: then let the Lord lead you." Perhaps you'll find conviction as to your own salvation. If that would be the case, why not make that a sure and real thing for yourself right now? Believe that Christ died for your sins, was buried, and was raised again for your justification: put your total trust in His finished work and receive the gift of eternal life…do it now.

Your approach to these pages should include your King James Bible at your side and believe what you can prove in scripture. The prayers of thousands of saints are with you as you study. You will be blessed and edified, of that I'm sure.

Faith of Christ

INTRODUCTION

THE GOOD LIFE

Picture this: a house on a beautiful lake, snuggled in a peaceful valley; a winding river that flows through the center of town; a community of people who genuinely care for each other; a governing body whose one desire is to please you and honor you; a police force whose main purpose is to assist you any way they can as there is no crime; streets that glisten in the light because they are so clean; and beautiful music on every street corner; happy sounds everywhere you go, no Mister Scrooge, no locks on your doors, no bills to pay – only serenity!

It's difficult to believe that there might be a place like that, isn't it? But there is such a place, only better. There is no way our finite minds can comprehend what God has in store for those of us who love Him and have trusted His Son as our Savior. That is how eternity with God will be, beautiful beyond imagination and comprehension. What is even more amazing is all of this was provided for you and me long before we were conceived in our mother's womb.

It is difficult to believe that before I was ever born someone would do something for me that would ensure me of a retirement free from all indebtedness, plus guarantee me satisfaction and happiness. However, God has done that and Jesus Christ is our assurance of that reward. As a matter of fact, Christ and Christ alone is the guarantor. You cannot buy this retirement plan, neither can you get it because you know somebody or because you know somebody who knows somebody. You cannot get this retirement because you won the world contest for being the kindest, sweetest, easiest to get along with, most compatible person in the entire world.

Entry into God's retirement community is free! Jesus Christ paid the price for those who are its inhabitants. He paid the price the gatekeeper of this community, God, demanded. Christ paid for it over 2,000 years ago and he has offered it to all who will accept God's conditions for occupancy. The conditions are so simple many think they are too good to be true, so they refuse the offer, they refuse the gift.

BAD LIFE

Because people refuse the offer of a good life, their retirement community will be drastically different. Instead of a quiet, peaceful atmosphere; theirs will be one of pain and agony. The people who live in this community will never live in peace and harmony. They will never enjoy the sounds of beautiful music. The sounds they will hear will be those of fellow citizens crying out in torment because all peoples in this community will be in constant pain day and night. The people will cry out and ask God to be merciful and kill them so they can be free from this torment, but their cries will be in vain. They will not die.

People who have journeyed to this retirement community must live here for all eternity without any hope of escaping. They will have to learn to ignore the smell of rotting flesh. They will become indifferent to the decayed bodies of all inhabitants, for all who live here will have the stench of a body unattended by a funeral director. The pain of the people will be so intense they will grind their teeth together, making a noise that is annoying to all who hear, and believe me, all will hear. Sleep will not come here, because the torment is constant. There is no beauty in this place, only ugliness; no joy, only sorrow. This retirement community will be the most disgusting place in all of creation.

The reason someone would choose this kind of retirement is hard for us to understand, but many will choose this life because they refuse to believe in God and want no part of the promises he has in store for all those who do believe in Jesus Christ.

Perhaps you might be thinking, "I have never made that choice." But you have. You made the choice when you refused to accept the free gift Christ offered you. God does not force one to accept His life-style. He does not use media bombardment or crafty sales techniques that his opponents do. God's Word, The Holy Bible, says, "Here is my Son, Jesus Christ. Accept what He did for you: died for your sins, was buried and then resurrected, and you will inherit life everlasting with Me."

Refusal to accept what God requires means automatic entrance into the other retirement community.

We want to explore with you what God has required, over the various dispensations of time, to be a participant in the Good Life.

1. God's Plan

Long before He created the world, God made provisions for man to share eternity with Him: Jesus Christ would come to earth to die for the sins of fallen man. Even though man had not fallen yet, God, who is omniscient (all knowing), knew that He would create Adam, that Adam would disobey the command of God, thus committing a sin, and he would be in need of a Savior. Everyone who would be born into this new world would be the direct descendant of sinful Adam, would be of the seed of Adam, and be born with the sin of Adam.

Even though Adam was created in the image of God: **"So God created man in his own image, in the image of God created he him; male and female created he them."** Genesis 1: 27; when he and Eve had their first child, he was born in the image of fallen Adam. **"And Adam lived an hundred and thirty years, and begat a son <u>in his own likeness</u>, after his image; and called his name Seth:"** Genesis 5: 3.

Since God knows all things, he made preparations and provisions for all who would accept Christ:

1. All who would accept Christ as Savior would look like Christ.
2. He would send the Holy Spirit to call those who would acccpt and draw them unto Him.
3. Once they "heeded" the call, He would justify them (not let their sin be a barrier anymore).
4. Then He would glorify them and they would be like God.

Romans 8: 28-30:

> **28. And we know that all things work together for good to them that love God, to them who are the called according to his purpose.**
> **29. For whom he did foreknow, he also did predestinate to be conformed to the image of his Son, that he might be the firstborn among many brethren.**
> **30. Moreover whom he did predestinate, them he also called: and whom he called, them he also justified: and whom he justified, them he also glorified.**

All of these things were <u>provided</u> for mankind but not <u>decided</u> for them. Man must make the choice to choose Christ, but once he does then Romans 8: 28-30 becomes operational: man will be conformed to the image of the Son of God, will be justified and glorified.

In making these provisions, God is not only showing His intentions, but proving to everyone His veracity by following through. God's plan for mankind's salvation was and is simple. All God would require of man would be simple faith in the faith of Christ.

Today, man has a choice:

1. To do what God requires and live with Him forever.
2. Not do what God requires and live in another world, apart from God.

Let us explore some of the requirements of God.

1.

THE FAITH THAT WAS IN THE OLD TESTAMENT

ABEL'S FAITH

Rebellion against the command of God was the cause of Adam's sin and subsequent fall. When Adam sinned, God killed an animal and made Adam and Eve a covering for their nakedness: **"Unto Adam also and to his wife did the LORD God make coats of skins, and clothed them."** Genesis 3: 21.

This is the first time that a sacrifice was recorded in the Scripture. It established a precedent and a requirement for rebellious and sinful man: THERE MUST BE A BLOOD SACRIFICE PROVIDED FOR REMISSION OF SINS. Eradication of sin must come from the blood of the Redeemer, Jesus Christ.

NOTE: The blood of animals was for remission of sins for the past year. It was not for the blotting out of sins. "**For it is not possible that the blood of bulls and of goats should take away sins.**" Hebrews 10:4. There is a difference between the temporal remission of sins and those sins being blotted out.

When we get to the fourth chapter of Genesis we are introduced to Cain and Able, the sons of Adam and Eve. There is no question but that these two sons knew the requirement of a sacrifice for their sins.

Genesis 4:

> **2. And in process of time it came to pass, that Cain brought of the fruit of the ground an offering unto the LORD.**
> **3. And Abel, he also brought of the firstlings of his flock and of the fat thereof. And the LORD had respect unto Abel and to his offering:**
> **4. But unto Cain and to his offering he had not respect. And Cain was very wroth, and his countenance fell.**
> **5. And the LORD said unto Cain, Why art thou wroth? and why is thy countenance fallen?**
> **6. <u>If thou doest well</u>, shalt thou not be accepted? and if thou doest not well, sin lieth at the door. And unto thee shall be his desire, and thou shalt rule over him.**

Abel brings an animal sacrifice unto God, a blood sacrifice; Cain brings a sacrifice as well, but his was a bunch of fruit. God had established the animal sacrifice when He provided the coats of skin for Adam and Eve. Abel obeyed God and his sacrifice was accepted. Cain did not obey God and his sacrifice was rejected. Cain made an attempt to *substitute* a non-blood sacrifice and God would not accept it, so Cain got a little upset.

Granted, the fruit was the very best that Cain had to offer, but the simple fact was that God required a different sacrifice. Faith does what God requires, at the time God requires it. Anything else, regardless of how good it may be, is not acceptable to God.

Able offered exactly what God required and his sacrifice was accepted.

"By faith Abel offered unto God a <u>more excellent</u> sacrifice than Cain, by which he obtained witness that he was righteous, God testifying of his gifts: and by it he being dead yet speaketh." Hebrews 11: 4.

God said: "Offer the right sacrifice and you will be accepted (saved; offer the wrong sacrifice and you will be rejected (not saved/lost)."

Cain could have offered the sacrifice God required and God would have welcomed it along with Cain, Genesis 4: 7 is clear about that. Look at it again.

<u>If thou doest well</u>, shalt thou not be accepted? and if thou doest not well, sin lieth at the door. And unto thee shall be his desire, and thou shalt rule over him.

Cain did exactly what he wanted to do with no regard for what God wanted him to do, and then he got upset with God because the Lord did not think his sacrifice was good enough. Because Cain was stubborn, prideful and unwilling to accept the requirement of God; his sacrifice was refused and Cain became a friend of the god of this world (Satan) and consequently an enemy of God.

"Ye adulterers and adulteresses, know ye not that the friendship of the world is enmity with God? whosoever therefore will be a friend of the world is the enemy of God." James 4: 4.

Mankind has ignored the lesson taught here in Genesis, for man has been trying to make substitutions, just as Cain did, for what God has required for salvation ever since that notable day of Cain's failure.

There are "religious systems" built around substitutionary offerings this very day. You may be a part of one of them and not even know it. (We will cover this in detail in later chapters.)

Abel offered the required sacrifice and it was pleasing to God. His faith, in offering the sacrifice which God required, was his salvation. He simply did as God required of him and became acceptable to God. That is what faith does. Faith does whatever God says to do at the time He requires it done.

ENOCH

There is very little written about Enoch, but there is enough for us to see that Enoch was a man that did what God said to do:

"By faith Enoch was translated that he should not see death; and was not found, because God had translated him: for before his translation he had this testimony, that he pleased God." Hebrews 11: 5.

Wouldn't it be great if God could say we pleased Him? That is all he wants from us. Is it too much to ask considering all He has done for us?

Enoch did whatever God said do, and that pleased God. Because he was obedient to what God asked from him, God took Enoch home with Him. In other words, God saved him and transported him to live with Him forever.

NOAH

By the time Noah had reached the ripe old age of 500, the world was a pretty rotten place. God saw that the wickedness of man was great in that every thought of mankind was to do evil things continually, and God would have destroyed all of mankind, but for Noah.

"**And GOD saw that the wickedness of man was great in the earth, and that every imagination of the thoughts of his heart was only evil continually. And it repented the LORD that he had made man on the earth, and it grieved him at his heart. And the LORD said, I will destroy man whom I have created from the face of the earth; both man, and beast, and the creeping thing, and the fowls of the air; for it repenteth me that I have made them. But Noah found grace in the eyes of the LORD.**" Genesis 6: 5-8.

God told Noah what He wanted him to do:

"**By faith Noah, being warned of God of things not seen as yet, moved with fear, prepared an ark to the saving of his house; by the which he condemned the world, and became heir of the righteousness which is by faith.**" Hebrews 11: 7.

We have already said that faith will do whatever God says do. In the case of Noah, God said: "Build me an ark and I will save you and your household." What did faith do? Faith, moved with fear, built an ark to the saving of his house. Because of this act of faith, the building of the ark as instructed, God declared Noah to be righteous (a child of God).

It should be getting very clear to you by now: "If you want to please God, you need to do what He requires of you for the time in which you live."

ABRAHAM

God required Abraham to do certain things for his salvation, just as he required it of Able, Enoch and Noah. God established certain things for Abraham to perform in order to test his obedience. The following are but two of those requirements:

1. God said: "**Now the LORD had said unto Abram, Get thee out of thy country, and from thy kindred, and from thy father's house, unto a land that I will shew thee:**" Genesis 12:1. He left, not knowing where he was going. "**By faith Abraham, when he was called to go out into a place which he should after receive for an inheritance, obeyed; and he went out, not knowing whither he went.**" Hebrews 11: 8.
2. God said, "I want you to offer your son Isaac as a sacrifice." Abraham prepared to do so, for he had faith that God would raise him from the dead. "**By faith Abraham, when he was tried, offered up Isaac: and he that had received the promises offered up his only begotten son, Of whom it was said, That**

in Isaac shall thy seed be called: Accounting that God was able to raise him up, even from the dead; from whence also he received him in a figure." Hebrews 11: 17-19.

Abraham was rewarded for his faithfulness and is known as the father of many, even though he had become a very old man when Sarah conceived Isaac. **"Therefore sprang there even of one, and him as good as dead, so many as the stars of the sky in multitude, and as the sand which is by the sea shore innumerable."** Hebrews 11: 12.

Abraham was ninety-nine years old when Isaac was conceived, but he believed God and did what God asked of him. Because of his faith, Abraham was blessed of God and thereby assured that his seed would be many; for through the seed of Isaac and Jacob Jesus was born, in whom all the world would be blessed.

Abraham did all that God asked of him, believing that God would do all that He said He would do. His faith and his actions (works) were pleasing to God, and God counted it to him for righteousness. **"For what saith the scripture? Abraham believed God, and it was counted unto him for righteousness."** Romans 4: 3.

In the eleventh chapter of Hebrews there are many names listed in "The Faith Hall of Fame). But time and space will only permit us to add two more: Moses and Rahab.

MOSES

In the time that Herod was the leader over Israel, he decreed that all male children born of the Hebrew women were to be killed. Moses' parents knew there was something special about their newborn son, so they hid him for three months after birth before putting him in a place where he was sure to be found. Pharaoh's daughter spotted the little one while bathing in the river and took him home with her, where he was raised in the house of Pharaoh.

When Moses became a man, he refused to be called the son of Pharaoh's daughter. **"Choosing rather to suffer affliction with the people of God, than to enjoy the pleasures of sin for a season;"** Hebrews 11: 25.

God called Moses to lead the children of Israel out of Egypt. Many know a lot about the plagues that God inflicted on the Egyptians but the most significant one was when God told Moses to have his people sprinkle the blood of an animal over the door and on the side post of their dwelling place, and if they would do so, the first born male of their household would live rather than die. (Exodus 12). By faith, Moses instructed the people, and those who did as the Lord required, were spared their lives when the death angle passed over the land that night. God spared the lives of all those who obeyed His command.

By faith, Moses and the children of Israel walked through the Red Sea on dry land, but those of Pharaoh's army were swallowed up by the water. (Exodus 14).

Moses, just like those of faith before him, did whatever God told him to do; and God did for Moses as He had done for those before him – saved him and counted the works he did for righteousness.

RAHAB

The story concerning Rahab is a most interesting one; you will find it detailed in the Book of Joshua – Chapters 2 through 6.

Rahab was a harlot (Joshua 2: 1). Joshua sent two spies to scope out Jericho and they came to Rahab's house. Even though the King of Jericho had sent messages to Rahab to turn the spies over to him, she did not, choosing to hide them instead and also to lie concerning there whereabouts (Joshua 2: 1-4). Rahab later told the two men that she knew the Lord had already given them the land and asked them to spare her and her family.

The only way she could have known Jericho would be taken was if God had revealed it unto her. So when Joshua gave orders to destroy the city and its inhabitants, he excluded Rahab and her family: **"And the city shall be accursed, even it, and all that are therein, to the LORD: only Rahab the harlot shall live, she and all that are with her in the house, because she hid the messengers that we sent."** Joshua 6: 17.

Rahab and her family were saved because they did as God instructed them to do. **"Likewise also was not Rahab the harlot justified by works, when she had received the messengers, and had sent them out another way?"** James 2: 25

SUMMARY

In the old Testament, if one was to be declared righteous, one would simply do what God said do.

1. If God said, "Cain and Able, offer an animal sacrifice." Faith would offer an animal sacrifice. Abel did and was declared righteous; Cain did not and was not declared righteous, but was cursed of God.
2. If God said, "Enoch, do what I say do." Faith would do whatever God said. Apparently Enoch did just that, for the Scripture says "He pleased God." "**By faith Enoch was translated that he should not see death; and was not found, because God had translated him: for before his translation he had this testimony, that <u>he pleased God</u>**." Hebrews 11:5. And we know God took Enoch home with Him.
3. If God said: "Noah, build me an ark and I will save you and your house"; faith would build an ark. That's exactly what Noah did and God kept His promise.
4. If God said: "Abraham, get thee out of thy country, be circumcised and offer your only begotten son Isaac as a sacrifice"; What would faith do but get out, be circumcised and offer Isaac as a sacrifice? Abraham did all those things and they were counted to him for righteousness.
5. If God said: "Moses, put the blood over your door and on the side post and I will save your first born son; then walk across the Red Sea on dry land and I will save you." Faith would do it, without hesitation. Moses did all that was asked of Him and God saved him.
6. If God said: "Rahab, hide the two messengers of God and send those looking for them away and I will save you and your house"; faith would hide the men. Rahab did that and God saved her as well as her family.

It is faith and faith alone that saved the Old Testament saints. Faith obeys whatever God requires for the time at hand. The

Scriptures are clear about that. There is no better explanation of what we just said than is found in James 2: 20-26:

20. But wilt thou know, O vain man, that faith without works is dead?
21. Was not Abraham our father justified by works, when he had offered Isaac his son upon the altar?
22. Seest thou how faith wrought with his works, and by works was faith made perfect?
23. And the scripture was fulfilled which saith, Abraham believed God, and it was imputed unto him for righteousness: and he was called the Friend of God.
24. Ye see then how that by works a man is justified, and not by faith only.
25. Likewise also was not Rahab the harlot justified by works, when she had received the messengers, and had sent them out another way?
26. For as the body without the spirit is dead, so faith without works is dead also.

Old Testament faith had to be followed with the response of a work being performed by the individual. There is no way to separate one from the other. In Old Testament times there would not have been an evidence of faith apart from works.

Do not be confused by this. We will show in subsequent passages that individual works are no longer a part of the salvation process. But for the period of time under discussion faith must be followed by works.

3.

THE FAITH THAT WAS: IN THE GOSPELS

Webster's dictionary defines "righteous" as: meeting the standards of what is right and just.

With respect to Israel, the chosen people of God through the seed of Abraham, Isaac and Jacob, one was made righteous if he did as God demanded or commanded him. One's sins would be taken care of <u>temporarily</u> until the time when those sins would be blotted out permanently by the blood of Christ. This blotting out of sins for Israel and all the saved of the Old Testament and the four Gospels as well, will take place after Christ sets up His 1,000 year millennial reign. It did not happen the moment they confessed Christ as the Messiah. (We will show you when that started later on in the booklet.)

In the Old Testament we saw God demanding certain works in order to be declared righteous. What we must address at this time is: Does all that change with the coming of Christ? The question is: "Are works by man still required in Matthew, Mark, Luke and John in order to be approved of God"? The answer is, yes!

With the coming of John the Baptist we see the introduction of a new work – water baptism. In Luke 3: 3 we see the following: **"And he came into all the country about Jordan, preaching the baptism of repentance for the remission of sins;"** The passage is about John the Baptist preaching that one must be baptized in order to have remission of sins.

What does that mean exactly? It means that a new requirement for righteousness is being introduced. It means that God now requires a person to be baptized if they are to be accepted of Him. It is a work that has to be done. It is no different from the work of circumcision, the building of an arc or the offering of an animal sacrifice for the remission of sins.

I want you to examine the word "remission" for a moment. When we say that a particular disease, like cancer, is in remission; does that mean it no longer exists? It generally means the disease has only been arrested momentarily and there is a possibility that it may re-appear. We will discuss this in more detail later, but I want you to think of what I just said as we continue with our commentary.

In the third chapter of the Book of Matthew, we find John the Baptist speaking to a group of people. He tells them that he comes baptizing with water unto repentance, but Christ will come and baptize them with the Holy Ghost and with fire. **"I indeed baptize you with water unto repentance: but he that cometh after me is mightier than I, whose shoes I am** not worthy to bear: he shall baptize you with the Holy Ghost, and with fire:"** Matthew 3: 11.

Not too long after this event took place, Jesus comes before John, requesting to be baptized. John says, "That should not happen, Lord, you need to baptize me, not I you."

Look at the Lord's response: **"And Jesus answering said unto him, Suffer it to be so now: for thus it becometh us to fulfil all righteousness. Then he suffered him."** Matthew 3: 15.

Now what do you suppose the meaning of the words, "to fulfil all righteousness" means? Jesus tells John it is necessary for Him, the Lord, to be baptized to fulfil all righteous. Just as Old Testament saints were to perform certain works before they were declared righteous, Jesus is saying He must do what is required in order that He might fulfil the righteous command for that day and age.

Would it not stand to reason that if God had some specific requirements for those living in the time period we are now discussing, all who wished to please God would comply? Sure it would. Look at the following passage that elude to that thought.

Jesus saith unto them, My meat is to do the will of him that sent me, and to finish his work. John 4: 34.

I can of mine own self do nothing: as I hear, I judge: and my judgment is just; because I seek not mine own will, but the will of the Father which hath sent me. John 5: 30.

Jesus answered them, and said, My doctrine is not mine, but his that sent me. John 7: 16.

And he that sent me is with me: the Father hath not left me alone; for I do always those things that please him. John 8: 29.

These verses spoken by Jesus tell of the Savior seeking only to please God and to do God's will. So, if the will of the Father was for all to be baptized, Jesus would be baptized, thus fulfilling all righteousness.

Unlike all others of that time period, Jesus was not baptized for the remission of sins, for He had no sin; He was simply doing the will of the Father. God said do it. He did it. God demanded obedience to His commands; Jesus was obedient and was baptized.

Baptism, like circumcision was never intended to blot out one's sins. Baptism was a temporal cleansing until the blood of Jesus would blot out all sins. If God said: "Be baptized and your sins will be remitted until the time of restitution when they will be blotted out", faith would be baptized expecting the blotting out of their sins to be forthcoming.

Jesus was baptized simply because God required it for that time period. His purpose was to please God and do His will. That was no difference from the requirements God imposed on Old Testament saints.

But His baptism was for another purpose in the fulfilling of all righteousness also. In Old Testament days the priest would wash the animal sacrifice before offering it on the altar of sacrifice. Jesus' baptism was in fulfillment of that. It was in preparation for His own sacrifice: His death on Calvary.

WHAT ABOUT AFTER THE DEATH OF CHRIST?

Were works still operational in order to fulfill all righteousness? Did the requirements of God change once Christ died? No, they did not!. In the command Jesus gave His disciples after His resurrection, we read these words:

"Go ye therefore, and teach all nations, baptizing them in the name of the Father, and of the Son, and of the Holy Ghost: Teaching them to observe all things whatsoever I have commanded you: and, lo, I am with you alway, even unto the end of the world. Amen." Matthew 28: 1920.

"And he said unto them, Go ye into all the world, and preach the gospel to every creature. He that believeth and is baptized shall be saved; but he that believeth not shall be damned." Mark 16: 15-16.

In the following passages, the Lord has already gone back to be with the Father, and there doesn't appear to be any change in what the apostles are preaching.

"Now when they heard this, they were pricked in their heart, and said unto Peter and to the rest of the apostles, Men and brethren, what shall we do? Then Peter said unto them, Repent, and be baptized every one of you in the name of Jesus Christ for the remission of sins, and ye shall receive the gift of the Holy Ghost." Acts 2: 37-38.

There are some who say there was a big change. They will tell you that in Matthew and Mark the command was to baptize in the name of the Father, Son and Holy Ghost, whereas in Acts they are commanded to baptize in the name of Jesus Christ. The fact remains that baptism was still a requirement and that is the subject we are presently discussing.

What is sad is that there are those that based their entire religious belief over the fact that one must be baptized in Jesus' name or they will not be saved. They have missed the point entirely that baptism never saved, it was only a temporal thing, a work that must be performed at that time in order to please God.

If God said: "Repent and be baptized for the remission of sins:; faith would do that. Baptism was as much a work as:

1. The animal sacrifices of Abel.
2. The work Enoch did to please God.
3. The building of the ark by Noah.
4. The getting out of the country, being circumcised, and the offering of Isaac by Abraham.
5. The putting of the blood on the door and walking across the Red Sea by Moses.
6. The hiding of the messengers by Rahab.

There is not one bit of difference. So we can add to our list of works.

7. The baptism of repentance for the remission of sins from John the Baptist up until the Dispensation of Grace.

Baptism is as much a work as the other six were. It is something *you* must do. It is something people can see. Yet, baptism was not something new, nor was it begun by John the Baptist as some suggest. It only became a requirement for remission of sins when God instructed John to teach it.

The practice of washing (baptizing) the sacrifice was already established under the law.

"Then verily the first covenant had also ordinances of divine service, and a worldly sanctuary." Hebrews 9: 1.

"Which was a figure for the time then present, in which were offered both gifts and sacrifices, that could not make him that did the service perfect, as pertaining to the conscience; Which stood only in meats and drinks, and divers washings (baptism)**, and carnal ordinances, imposed on them** (by the Law) **until the time of reformation."** Hebrews 9: 9-10.

Israel, God's covenant people, had so transgressed against God that John the Baptist was calling them to repentance and back to godly fellowship. Animal sacrificial washing was not good enough, they would now need to present themselves as clean (baptized) vessels before Almighty God. Thus the call of John was to repent and be baptized (cleansed) for the remission of your sins.

This baptism of oneself, taught by John, like the baptism of animals, was never intended to be the answer for salvation. It was a temporal thing. The purpose of John's baptism was to be cleansed temporarily until the times of refreshing came. (The second coming of Christ.)

"Then came together unto him the Pharisees, and certain of the scribes, which came from Jerusalem. ....And when they saw some of his disciples eat bread with defiled, that is to say, with unwashen, hands, they found fault. For the Pharisees, and all the Jews, except they wash their hands oft, eat not, holding the tradition of the elders. And when they come from the market, except they wash (the same word for baptize)**, they eat not. And many other things there be, which they have received to hold, as the**

washing of cups, and pots, brasen vessels, and of tables." Mark 7: 1, 3-4.

Baptism was an act of cleanliness. The animal sacrifice was washed (baptized) in order to present the sacrifice clean before the Lord. A priest washed (baptized) his hands before he accepted the animal sacrifice, and so on and so forth it goes.

But certain denominations have turned baptism into a religious issue. Let me try to get you to see what Jesus thought about that. Continue to read with me in Mark 7: 4-7: "**Then the Pharisees and scribes asked him, Why walk not thy disciples according to the tradition of the elders, but eat bread with unwashen** (un-baptized) **hands? He answered and said unto them, Well hath Esaias prophesied of you hypocrites, as it is written, This people honoureth me with their lips, but their heart is far from me. Howbeit in vain do they worship me, teaching for doctrines the commandments of men.**"

When an entire denomination is based upon the doctrine of baptism, is this not commandments of men? Religion is destroying Christianity. Religious organizations emphasize their own doctrinal issues rather than teaching people how to understand God's Word.

FACT: The way a denomination baptizes is not important in this Dispensation of Grace. You can sprinkle, immerse the whole body or just the head, and as far as God is concerned you are nothing more than the hypocritical Pharisees he chastised above. Baptism, like the law it was a part of, has been replaced by the grace of God.

Baptism was a work that men could boast about. "I've been baptized, have you? You haven't? Well if you haven't you are lost and going to hell."

Preachers talk to other preachers and say: "We baptized 50 people this quarter, how many baptisms did you have?" Shouldn't they be saying how many people got saved? Or do you suppose they think baptisms are synonymous with salvation? If so how do you justify the following

Ephesians 2: 8-9: **For by grace are ye saved through faith; and that not of yourselves: it is the gift of God: <u>Not of works, lest any man should boast.</u>**

4.

THE FAITH THAT IS – NOW

Most Christians will tell you that we are living in the age of grace or the Dispensation of Grace, but when asked to define what that is their answer is either weak or rote. For instance, they might say "It is a time when mankind is saved by the grace of God or it is a time that God is dealing graciously with man."

That is a true saying but a very weak answer in that it does not really cover the depth of God's purpose for this age. God has always dealt graciously with man in every generation and dispensation. However, this present Dispensation of Grace is the only time God has dealt with man without requiring man's work to be an integral part of the salvation process. Christ did the work for us when he shed His blood on Calvary. So, we are living in a dispensation where we are saved by grace through faith – NOT OF WORKS.

There are no animal sacrifices needed because God provided the perfect sacrifice – Jesus Christ. There is no baptism needed because we are cleansed by the blood of Christ. Many Christians know this but they have limited knowledge about the requirements of faith that came before the Dispensation of Grace and will come again when this dispensation reaches its end.

Question: If works were necessary prior to the law and during the Dispensation of the Law; and if works were necessary immediately after the resurrection and ascension of Christ, when did faith without works start?

Question: If Peter did not preach faith alone apart from works at Pentecost, who started preaching it?

Question: Is it all that important to know who started preaching this message of grace? Does it make any difference who started preaching it?

We think it does make a difference and we want you to know why.

BEWARE OF FALSE TEACHERS

It is appalling that the majority of Christians do not care enough about the importance of knowing the truth as well as their refusal to study the Bible in order to find the truth.

We have become a complacent society. We get upset more about lying politicians than we do about lying preachers. If we catch a politician in a lie we go to great lengths to make sure they are exposed and removed from office; but we won't even give one hour a day in studying God's word to prove what a preacher is teaching is wrong.

Why do you suppose that is true? Could it be there are so many of us who just do not care? Or could it be that we do not know enough about the Bible to even question their veracity? Perhaps both, but I would venture to say it is the latter and that is a most disturbing thought.

I believe that ninety percent of the people attending churches today get ninety-five percent of their knowledge of the Bible from what a preacher said the Scriptures said, not through searching the Scriptures to find what God really said.

Question: How do you know what your preacher is teaching is in fact truth? When the apostle Paul was evaluating two churches, listen to his praise for those at Berea and why he praised them.

"These were more noble than those in Thessalonica, in that they (1) received the word with all readiness of mind, and (2) searched the scriptures daily, whether those things were so." Acts 17: 11.

If we would be considered noble, based upon the criteria in Acts 17:11, we would:

1) Listen to what a preacher or teacher says and,
2) But we would not believe what was said without checking our Bibles first.
3) If what the preacher or teacher said is not the same as what the Bible says, do not believe the preacher or teacher.

And I say if the latter is true, you ought to quit listening to that person. He is a false teacher. We should make sure that the Scripture used to prove a point does not contradict with other Scripture. If there is a question as to whether or not there is a contradiction then you need to determine where that Scripture fits and into what dispensation it applies.

You need to get in the habit of asking questions. Such as, 1) To whom is the passage written, those under the law or those under grace. 2) In what time period does this Scripture refer: past dispensations or the present dispensation?

The Bible does not contradict itself, but false teachers will say it does when it does not agree with their doctrinal position, or when they are trying to get you to believe a lie.

Asking questions is a good way to study and to grow in understanding. Questioning a Bible teacher is a great way to determine their knowledge as well as there veracity. If a preacher or teacher will not tell the truth about one particular thing, he will not tell the truth about another and another. One lie leads to another lie.

The Bible warns us about these false teachers in 2 Corunthians11: 13-15:

"For such are false apostles, deceitful workers, transforming themselves into the apostles of Christ. And no marvel; for Satan himself is transformed into an angel of light. Therefore it is no great thing if his ministers also be transformed as the ministers of righteousness; whose end shall be according to their works."

If the word of God tells us: **"But before faith came, we were kept under the law, shut up unto the faith which should afterwards be revealed. Wherefore the law was our schoolmaster to bring us unto Christ, that we might be justified by faith. But after that faith is come, we are no longer under a schoolmaster."** Galatians 3: 23-25. Why do some preachers tell you that you are still under the law and must keep the ordinances of the law? They must be false teachers acting as though they are ministers of Christ.

If the word of God says: "**For by grace are ye saved through faith; and that not of yourselves: it is the gift of God: Not of works, lest any man should boast.**" Ephesians 2: 8-9; why do preachers say you have to be baptized or speak in tongues (which are works) to be saved? They must be false teachers acting as though they are ministers of Christ.

Paul was confronted with false teachers coming into an assembly after he had departed. Look what he says about them: **I marvel that ye are so soon removed from him that called you into the grace of Christ unto another gospel: Which is not another; but there be some that trouble you, and would pervert the gospel of Christ. But though we, or an angel from heaven, preach any other gospel unto you than that which we have preached unto you, let him be accursed.** Galatians 1: 6-8.

There are false teachers in pulpits today masquerading as minister of Christ. Their one objective is to deceive you into believing The Lie. Here are a few examples of what I mean:

1) Some give just enough truth so you will not question them. Remember our training from school when taking a true/false exam? Weren't you instructed that if one part of the statement was false then the whole statement was considered to be false? Yes!
2) Others act as though they are the sweetest thing this side of fresh honey, in the hope of your thinking they can do no wrong. There is an old saying that goes like this: "You catch more flies with honey than you do with vinegar." Watch out for the sweet ones.

3) Still others deceive you with their eloquence and charisma. Hitler was a charismatic individual and so was Jim Jones. Look at what happened to their followers.
4) Some even get you caught up in their deceit by the music they sing and the excitement it brings. What is their objective, to get you so worked up emotionally in singing you will not know or care what is being said? Now that's the best one yet.

Beware! Beware! Beware! Beware!

I am not saying that every charismatic, eloquent individual is a false person or that everyone who loves to sing is following untruth; nor am I saying that a man of God cannot be a sweet, loving and compassionate individual. I am only showing you the possibilities and the probabilities out there. If you are really interested in knowing the truth, always follow this suggestion from 1 Peter 5: 8: **"Be sober, be vigilant; because your adversary the devil, as a roaring lion, walketh about, seeking whom he may devour:"**

REGENERATION

In the introduction I stated it was very hard to believe someone cared enough for me to die for my sins; but God did and Jesus Christ was willing to be my sin offering. God cared enough to ask His only begotten Son to die for the sins of man. Jesus Christ cared enough that He was willing to go into hell so my sins would be forgiven.

Christ's death, and the blood He shed on Calvary, was for the sins of all men: before the law, under the law, under grace and after grace.

However, there is one question that haunts many believers today: when were sins blotted out or atoned for? There are two answers for that one question, but before we examine them we need to get a clearer understanding of the word atonement.

There are seven Jewish feast days, one of them is The Feast of Atonement. The first time it is mentioned is in Leviticus 23: 27-32.

> 20 Also on the tenth day of this seventh month there shall be a day of atonement: it shall be an holy convocation unto you; and ye shall afflict your souls, and offer an offering made by fire unto the LORD.
> 21 And ye shall do no work in that same day: for it is a day of atonement, to make an atonement for you before the LORD your God.
> 22 For whatsoever soul it be that shall not be afflicted in that same day, he shall be cut off from among his people.
> 23 And whatsoever soul it be that doeth any work in that same day, the same soul will I destroy from among his people.
> 24 Ye shall do no manner of work: it shall be a statute for ever throughout your generations in all your dwellings.
> 25 It shall be unto you a sabbath of rest, and ye shall afflict your souls: in the ninth day of the month at even, from even unto even, shall ye celebrate your sabbath.

Once a year, on the Day of Atonement, the children of Israel were to bring their animal sacrifices to the High Priest. The High Priest would receive the sacrificial animal and slit its throat, catch the blood in a vessel and then put the blood on the animal, symbolic for the blood being a covering for sin. Once this ritual was performed, all the sins of the past were "atoned for." Then the next year, on the Day of Atonement, they would repeat the process. They must do this each and every year of their lives.

When Christ died on the cross, the symbolic animal sacrifice was not needed anymore. That sacrifice was part of Jewish law, and Christ abolished the law in His flesh.

"Having abolished in his flesh the enmity, even the law of commandments contained in ordinances; for to make in himself of twain one new man, so making peace;" Ephesians 2: 15.

It is Christ's blood that atones for sins. The question is: "At what time does this atonement take place?" The answer is two fold.

1). At the conclusion of his Pentecostal address, Peter said the following in Acts 3: 19-21:

> **19 Repent ye therefore, and be converted, that your sins may be blotted out, when the times of refreshing shall come from the presence of the Lord;**
> **20 And he shall send Jesus Christ, which before was preached unto you:**
> **21 Whom the heaven must receive until the times of restitution of all things, which God hath spoken by the mouth of all his holy prophets since the world began.**

The passage states that the atonement will come when Jesus Christ returns the second time, known as the second coming of Christ. The times of refreshing will come during the 1,000 year millennial reign of Christ. Christ returns at the end of the seven years of tribulation and then established His 1,000 year earthly reign as King.

Peter is addressing a predominately Jewish crowd. Peter has been preaching **"Then Peter said unto them, Repent, and be baptized every one of you in the name of Jesus Christ for the remission of sins, and ye shall receive the gift of the Holy Ghost."** Acts 2: 38.

What Peter tells the people is they must repent, be cleansed (baptized) so that their sins will be in remission until the time comes when those sins will be blotted out.

2) In Romans 5: 9-11, Paul is addressing a different group of believers, which we will call the Church the Body of Christ. Look at what he tells them:

> **9 Much more then, being <u>now</u> justified by his blood, we shall be saved from wrath through him.**
> **10 For if, when we were enemies, we were reconciled to God by the death of his Son, much more, being reconciled, we shall be saved by his life.**
> **11 And not only so, but we also joy in God through our Lord Jesus Christ, by whom we have <u>now</u> received the atonement.**

I want you to look at two parts of the passage above. In verse 9 you see the words, "shall be saved from wrath'; and in verse 11 the words "we have now received the atonement".

So, members of the Church the Body of Christ will not go through the wrath, which is the tribulation and the wrath to come, and their sins are atoned for NOW.

Are Acts 3:19-21 and Romans 5: 9-11 paradoxes, seemingly contradictory statements that may nonetheless be true? Yes they are! They are both truth, however, they speak to two different groups of people. The passages do not contradict. They are for two different dispensations and two separate time periods and are for two different groups of people.

Acts 3:19-21 is for Israel and all those who were saved under the Kingdom message preached by Peter. Their sins will be atoned when Christ returns to earth the second time. Whereas Romans 5: 9-11 is for the Church the Body of Christ and those who were saved by grace. Their sins are atoned the moment they trust Christ as their Savior.

SALVATION FOR ISRAEL

Let's look at Acts 3: 21 again: "**Whom the heaven must receive until the times of restitution of all things, which God hath spoken by the mouth of all his holy prophets since the world began.**" What prophets spoke of this event can be seen in Jeremiah 31:31-34. Lets go there.

> 31 Behold, the days come, saith the LORD, that I will make a new covenant with the house of Israel, and with the house of Judah:
> 32 Not according to the covenant that I made with their fathers in the day that I took them by the hand to bring them out of the land of Egypt; which my covenant they brake, although I was an husband unto them, saith the LORD:

33 But this shall be the covenant that I will make with the house of Israel; After those days, saith the LORD, I will put my law in their inward parts, and write it in their hearts; and will be their God, and they shall be my people.

34 And they shall teach no more every man his neighbour, and every man his brother, saying, Know the LORD: for they shall all know me, from the least of them unto the greatest of them, saith the LORD: for I will forgive their iniquity, and I will remember their sin no more.

Let us look very closely at what we just read.

1. V. 31 states there will be a New Covenant established with the house of Israel and the house of Judah. Judah is in reference to the two faithful tribes: Judah and Benjamin; and Israel is in reference to the ten unfaithful tribes.

2. V. 32: This New Covenant is different from the Old Covenant made with Israel, through Moses.

3. V. 33 says that God will put His law in their inward parts and write it on their hearts. In this dispensation, Israel's heart has been hardened because they went a whoring from the presence of God. **"My people ask counsel at their stocks, and their staff declareth unto them: for the spirit of whoredoms hath caused them to err, and they have <u>gone a whoring</u> from under their God."** Hosea 5: 12. God finally "put His foot down" and declared Israel to be Lo-ami, not my people. **"Be it known therefore unto you, that the salvation**

of God is sent unto the Gentiles, and that they will hear it." Acts 28: 28.

4. V. 33 also says, "I will be their God and they shall be my people." God will unlock their hardened hearts and bring them from the state of being Lo-ami (Not my people) to the state of being His people. The promised restoration of Israel will be realized. Look at Acts 1: 6: **"When they therefore were come together, they asked of him, saying, Lord, wilt thou at this time restore again the kingdom to Israel?"**

The restoration of Israel was what they were looking for, but that time did not come. Look at what Jesus said: **"And he said unto them, It is not for you to know the times or the seasons, which the Father hath put in his own power."** Acts 1: 7. The disciples knew about the prophecy of Jeremiah and were anticipating the earthly kingdom. But that did not happen in Acts. It will happen when Christ returns to earth.

5. V. 34: When Christ establishes His earthly Kingdom, all Israel will know the Lord. It is obvious that they do not know Him at this time.

6. V. 34: When the earthly Kingdom is established the lord will blot out Israel's sins. But for now, they are waiting for that day. All the saved of the Old Testament and all those who believed the Kingdom message that Peter preached are waiting for their Day of Atonement. It is a future event.

Fact: The Church the Body of Christ is not a New Covenant group of believers. The New Covenant is to be made with Israel and Judah. The New Covenant will become operational when Christ returns at the end of tribulation, establishes His 1,000 year millennial reign and sets up His earthly throne.

You have witnessed seemingly contradictory verse of Scripture, but if we learn to rightly divide the Word of Truth, as 2 Timothy 2: 15 states; **"Study to shew thyself approved unto God, a workman that needeth not to be ashamed, rightly dividing the word of truth."** We can see that the passages under consideration involves two separate dispensations.

SALVATION FOR THE CHURCH THE BODY OF CHRIST

Our salvation is by grace and not of works. We become a child of God by trusting in the Faith of Christ. What is the Faith of Christ? He believed the father would raise Him from the dead if he was willing to die for the sins of man.

> If you or I are saved today, it not because of anything we did.
>
> You/I cannot do anything to earn our salvation.
>
> You/I cannot do anything to make our salvation better or more meaningful.
>
> Your/My faith cannot save us; that would be a work.

You/I cannot add anything to what Christ has already done.

Look at Titus 3: 4-7: **"But after that the kindness and love of God our Saviour toward man appeared, <u>Not by works of righteousness which we have done</u>, but according to his mercy he saved us, by the washing of regeneration, and renewing of the Holy Ghost; Which he shed on us abundantly through Jesus Christ our Saviour; That being justified by his grace, we should be made heirs according to the hope of eternal life."**

THE FAITH OF CHRIST

The finished work of Christ means just what it says: "It is finished." It was finished the moment He rose from the dead and ascended into heaven. When we accept the finished work of Christ we die, and yet we are made alive: **"I am crucified with Christ: nevertheless I live; yet not I, but Christ liveth in me: and the life which I now live in the flesh I live by the faith of the Son of God, who loved me, and gave himself for me."** Galatians 2: 20.

This is another paradox: How can one be dead and still be alive? The Bible teaches we become a part of Christ's body the moment we believe the Gospel of Christ. Christ died; we died too. Christ rose from the dead; we rose from the dead too. By accepting the Faith of Christ we have been made alive spiritually, but dead to sin. That does not mean our flesh will not sin, it does. But it means that since Christ conquered sin, we will too, in resurrection.

If we believe that Christ did everything for our salvation and that we (mankind) can do nothing, and I do believe that; then the following Scriptures are very important for a clearing understanding of what we are saying. These verses of Scripture state our position without the need of a deep theological explanation.

Galatians 2:

> **16 I am crucified with Christ: nevertheless I live; yet not I, but Christ liveth in me: and the life which I now live in the flesh I live by the faith of the Son of God, who loved me, and gave himself for me.**

Galatians 3:

> **19 But the scripture hath concluded all under sin, that the promise by faith of Jesus Christ might be given to them that believe.**

Romans 3:

> **20 Even the righteousness of God which is by faith of Jesus Christ unto all and upon all them that believe: for there is no difference:**

Philippians 3:

> **9 And be found in him, not having mine own righteousness, which is of the law, but that which is through the faith of Christ, the righteousness which is of God by faith:**

What do all of these verses have in common? In a King James Bible, it is the Faith of Christ. They tell me I am justified by the Faith of Christ, I am made righteous by the Faith of Christ, and I live by the Faith of Christ.

So, what exactly was the Faith of Christ? Christ, who left His throne in Glory, had faith that the Father would restore Him to the position He had before he became flesh and blood. He also had faith that if He were to die and go into hell for the sins of the world, God would not leave his soul in hell. That was the faith Christ had. He believed that God would do what He said He would do.

Christ became a human sacrifice for the world's sins. It was a work that He was willing to perform and it was that work that justified all of mankind. It is His faith that saves me. I can do nothing for my salvation; it was completed when Christ died over 2,000 years ago.

THE GOSPEL UNTO SALVATION

Since salvation was taken care of by the Lord Jesus Christ over 2,000 years ago, how can it be mine?

"For I am not ashamed of the gospel of Christ: for it is the power of God unto salvation to every one that believeth; to the Jew first, and also to the Greek." Romans 1: 16.

"So what is the Gospel of Christ," you ask? It is found in 1 Corinthians 15: 1-4:

> **1 Moreover, brethren, I declare unto you the gospel which I preached unto you, which also ye have received, and wherein ye stand;**

> **2 By which also ye are saved, if ye keep in memory what I preached unto you, unless ye have believed in vain.**
> **3 For I delivered unto you first of all that which I also received, how that Christ died for our sins according to the scriptures;**
> **4 And that he was buried, and that he rose again the third day according to the scriptures:**

There are a lot of people who believe that Christ died, was buried and rose again but are as lost as they can be. You might be one of those. The Bible says, "**Thou believest that there is one God; thou doest well: the devils also believe, and tremble.**" James 2: 19. But it is impossible for the devil to be saved and live with God eternally because God has already condemned him to a life in the lake of fire.

There are many who have spent their entire life going to church. They will tell you they have always been a Christian. They believe in God, Jesus Christ, Easter and Christmas, but that does not mean they are saved and that does not mean they are a Christian.

Every person in this world has to understand that they are sinners. They were born sinners and will die sinners. But if a sinner believes that Christ paid the price for their sins and trust what He did for them on Calvary, then they are Children of God.

Some things you should understand scripturally:

1. You are a sinner: "**For all have sinned, and come short of the glory of God;**" Romans 3:23. You need to understand you are lost before you will understand the need to be saved.

2. The penalty for sin: "**For the wages of sin is death; but the gift of God is eternal life through Jesus Christ our Lord.**" Romans 6: 23. Since you are a sinner, you should die, but Christ intervened on your behalf, if you will trust what He did.
3. The gospel of your salvation: "**Moreover, brethren, I declare unto you the gospel which I preached unto you, which also ye have received, and wherein ye stand; By which also ye are saved, if ye keep in memory what I preached unto you, unless ye have believed in vain. For I delivered unto you first of all that which I also received, how that Christ died for our sins according to the scriptures; And that he was buried, and that he rose again the third day according to the scriptures:**" 1 Corinthians 15: 1-4.
4. The free gift of God: "**For by grace are ye saved through faith; and that not of yourselves: it is the gift of God: Not of works, lest any man should boast.**" Ephesians 2: 8-9.

The power of God unto salvation is the Gospel of Christ. The gospel is not the death, burial and resurrection of Christ. The gospel is **Christ died for our sins**, was buried and resurrected.

Satan knew Christ did not die for his sins, for Satan's sin separated him permanently from God. He knows there is a God and he knows who the Son of God is too. He believes in them and you'd better believe he knows that Christ rose from the dead, because when Christ did that he conquered death and Satan's power of death. Look at Hebrews 2: 14: "**Forasmuch then as the children are partakers of flesh and blood, he also himself likewise took part of the same;**

that through death he might destroy him that had the power of death, that is, the devil;"

So you see, just believing in God, Jesus Christ and His death burial and resurrection does not save unless you believe all He did was for you and your sins. Christ died for your sins and you must accept His work for you if you are to be saved.

One other thing, the Gospel is the power of God UNTO salvation. Christ is our salvation. There is nothing you can do to earn this salvation for it is the gift of God. Salvation has always been available to you. Now all you must do is believe the Gospel. Once it become personal for you, you will become a part of Christ's body and His Spirit will dwell in you.

SECURE: CHRIST LIVING IN ME

"For by one Spirit are we all baptized into one body, whether we be Jews or Gentiles, whether we be bond or free; and have been all made to drink into one Spirit." 1 Corinthians 12: 13.

"Now ye are the body of Christ, and members in particular." 1 Corinthians 12: 27.

"To whom God would make known what is the riches of the glory of this mystery among the Gentiles; which is Christ in you, the hope of glory:" Colossians 1: 27.

Think about it, Christ living in you! And if He does, that guarantees you eternal life with Him. You are part of Christ's body and that means that wherever He is, you are. He is now sitting at the right hand of the Father:

"But God, who is rich in mercy, for his great love wherewith he loved us, Even when we were dead in sins, <u>hath quickened</u> us together with Christ, (by grace ye are saved;) And hath raised us up together, and made us sit together in heavenly places in Christ Jesus: That in the ages to come he might shew the exceeding riches of his grace in his kindness toward us through Christ Jesus. For by grace are ye saved through faith; and that not of yourselves: it is the gift of God: Not of works, lest any man should boast." Ephesians 2: 4-9.

I underlined the words hath quickened so that you would understand this is "past tense." That means I have already been raised up into heaven spiritually. My Spirit is already with Christ, who is in heaven.

How can one teach that you can loose your salvation if they read the Scriptures listed above? They must be false teachers acting as though they are ministers of Christ. Beware! Beware!

God knows everything so He would know I was going to sin after I believed, wouldn't He? Sure He would. So when Christ died for the sins of the world, He died for all those sins I would commit a hundred tomorrows from now as well as for the ones I committed yesterday.

This question remains: "Did Christ die for ALL my sins or not"? And the answer is and always has been a resounding yes. How do I know that? I know that because the Word of God says so.

"And ye are complete in him, which is the head of all principality and power: In whom also ye are circumcised with the circumcision made without hands, in putting off

the body of the sins of the flesh by the circumcision of Christ: Buried with him in baptism, wherein also ye are risen with him through the faith of the operation of God, who hath raised him from the dead. And you, being dead in your sins and the uncircumcision of your flesh, <u>hath he quickened together with him</u>, *<u>having forgiven you all trespasses</u>*; Blotting out the handwriting of ordinances that was against us, which was contrary to us, and took it out of the way, nailing it to his cross; And having spoiled principalities and powers, he made a shew of them openly, triumphing over them in it." Colossians 2: 10-15.

Christ has already quickened those who trusted Him and has already forgiven them ALL their trespasses. Then how can some preacher say if I sin I will loose my salvation? He must be a false teacher acting as though he was a minister of light. Beware! If you continue to listen to him you will be his roommate in hell.

GOOD WORKS vs. BAD WORKS

Sin does not rob me of eternal life with Christ, but sin does rob me of something. Sin robs me of my reward. A Christian can do things (works) that are bad as well as good. My bad works, things done in my flesh, will be burned and I will suffer loss, but I will not suffer my inheritance. My good works, things done in the Spirit, will stand the test of fire and I will receive a reward. Look at 1 Corinthians 3; 11-16:

> 11 For other foundation can no man lay than that is laid, which is Jesus Christ.
> 12 Now if any man build upon this foundation gold, silver, precious stones, wood, hay, stubble;

13 Every man's work shall be made manifest: for the day shall declare it, because it shall be revealed by fire; and the fire shall try every man's work of what sort it is.
14 If any man's work abide which he hath built thereupon, he shall receive a reward.
15 If any man's work shall be burned, he shall suffer loss: but he himself shall be saved; yet so as by fire.
16 Know ye not that ye are the temple of God, and that the Spirit of God dwelleth in you?

The gold, silver and precious stones of verse twelve are good works. When they are subjected to fire they are purified, not destroyed. The end result is reward. The "If we suffer, we shall also reign with him" of 2 Timothy 2: 12 could very well be the reward spoken of in 1 Corinthians.

The wood, hay and stubble of verse twelve are bad works. When they are subjected to fire they burn completely, they are destroyed. The child of God will suffer loss, but he will still be secure in Christ, as verse fifteen states.

There are many skeptics, or false teachers who might wonder why we did not include 1 Corinthians 3: 17 in our commentary. "**If any man defile the temple of God, him shall God destroy; for the temple of God is holy, which temple ye are.**"

Fact: This body can be destroyed. It will be before we ascend into heaven, but God may also allow it to be delivered into the hands of Satan at anytime it ceases to be productive. Look at 2 Corinthians 5: 5: "**To deliver such an one unto Satan for the destruction of the flesh, that the spirit may be saved in the day of the Lord Jesus.**"

Good and bad works are contrasted with the spirit and the flesh. The two are not compatible. There is a war going on between the flesh and the Spirit and often times it is very frustrating for the believer. Look at what God's Word say on the subject.

"For the flesh lusteth against the Spirit, and the Spirit against the flesh: and these are contrary the one to the other: so that ye cannot do the things that ye would." Galatians 5: 17.

"For I know that in me (that is, in my flesh,) dwelleth no good thing: for to will is present with me; but how to perform that which is good I find not. For the good that I would I do not: but the evil which I would not, that I do. Now if I do that I would not, it is no more I that do it, but sin that dwelleth in me. I find then a law, that, when I would do good, evil is present with me. For I delight in the law of God after the inward man: But I see another law in my members, warring against the law of my mind, and bringing me into captivity to the law of sin which is in my members. O wretched man that I am! who shall deliver me from the body of this death? I thank God through Jesus Christ our Lord. So then with the mind I myself serve the law of God; but with the flesh the law of sin." Romans 7: 18-25.

Paul, the author of both Galatians and Romans, was aware of the battle of the flesh and the Spirit. He had problems with his flesh too. He was constantly fighting to overcome the desires of his flesh. But at least he was trying, unlike the majority of us who call ourselves Christians. We seem to be content with the fact that we are saved and already seated in heavenly places and go about living like children of the devil, rather than walk as children of God. Watch out! God could turn you over to Satan for the destruction of your flesh.

"But don't we have liberty under grace, as stated in Galatians 5: 1: **Stand fast therefore in the liberty wherewith Christ hath made us free, and be not entangled again with the yoke of bondage.**" one might say?

Yes! But you need to look at Galatians 5: 13: "**For, brethren, ye have been called unto liberty; only use not liberty for an occasion to the flesh, but by love serve one another.**" We must not abuse the liberty we have or we will prostitute the grace of God.

WHAT REGENERATION IS NOT TODAY

Regeneration in the Dispensation of Grace is not works performed by mankind. Salvation has always been accompanied with works, regardless of the dispensation. That is why proponents of it today quote James 2: 20: **"But wilt thou know, O vain man, that faith without works is dead?"** or James 2: 26: **"For as the body without the spirit is dead, so faith without works is dead also."** The works James speaks of are those that man can do.

There was a time when this statement applied to the believer. But in the Dispensation of Grace, in which we currently reside, man's work plays no part in salvation. The work that must be done has already been done by Christ.

1. Able had to offer the right sacrifice or not be accepted of God.
2. Noah had to build an ark before he and his family could be saved.

3. Abraham had to offer Isaac or not be declared righteous.
4. Moses had to put blood over the door so the first born male child could be saved. He also had to walk through the Red Sea to be saved.
5. Rahab had to send those looking for the men of God in another direction so that she and her family would be saved.
6. Those believer in the gospels had to repent and be baptized before they could be saved.

All these works were necessary because God said do them to show your faith. So then BY their faith, plus doing the required work, God saved them. Salvation has always been doing what God required, at the time He required them to be done.

Well, God does not require you to perform any work today. God says that people living in the Dispensation of Grace CANNOT DO ANYTHING that will save them. Let me be more emphatic, you MUST NOT DO ANYTHING in an attempt to be saved or you will frustrate the grace of God.

Salvation in the twenty-first century is a free gift, given by God because of the WORK of His Son. So then, the work that had been necessary for man to perform has been replaced by the work that Christ performed. **"For by grace are ye saved through faith; and that not of yourselves: it is the gift of God: Not of works, lest any man should boast."** Ephesians 2: 8-9.

Why would God say, **"and that not of yourselves"** if it had not once been of yourselves? In prior dispensations, salvation was BY faith doing whatever God said do. It was man's faith doing what God required at the time.

In this present dispensation it is all about Christ's faith that saves, and Christ has already done what was necessary: He died for the sins of the world; he became the sacrifice for sins. Salvation for this age involves the work of Christ.

Those of us living today cannot perform any work, cannot add anything to Christ's finished work. Persons in prior dispensations were saved **BY** their faith, accompanied with works. In the present dispensation, we receive our salvation **THROUGH** faith believing in Christ's faith and His work. Look at Romans 3: 30: "**Seeing it is one God, which shall justify the circumcision by faith, and uncircumcision through faith.**"

God has always required a work (by man) to follow an act of faith in every dispensation, with the exception of the dispensation of Grace. In this present dispensation Christ has done the work necessary. We must accept, through faith, the work of Christ for our salvation.

The uncircumcision of Romans 3:30 speaks of the Church the Body of Christ. This body of believers is a unique group of people, chosen in God before the foundation of the world.

"**According as he hath chosen us in him before the foundation of the world, that we should be holy and without blame before him in love:**" Ephesians 1: 4.

"**That in the ages to come he might shew the exceeding riches of his grace in his kindness toward us through Christ Jesus.**" Ephesians 2: 7.

The Bible says that the Church the Body of Christ will be an example to the world of the grace of God. For the first and only time, God is not requiring works of man as a show of faith. He allowed Christ to perform the work for us. That, my friend, is what grace is about. God has given us a precious gift, the gift of life through Christ Jesus our Lord. He died, became the sacrifice for sins, thus performing the work necessary to please God.

Let us look at James 2: 20-26:

> **20 But wilt thou know, O vain man, that faith without works is dead?**
> **21 Was not Abraham our father justified by works, when he had offered Isaac his son upon the altar?**
> **22 Seest thou how faith wrought with his works, and by works was faith made perfect?**
> **23 And the scripture was fulfilled which saith, Abraham believed God, and it was imputed unto him for righteousness: and he was called the Friend of God.**
> **24 Ye see then how that by works a man is justified, and not by faith only.**
> **25 Likewise also was not Rahab the harlot justified by works, when she had received the messengers, and had sent them out another way?**
> **26 For as the body without the spirit is dead, so faith without works is dead also.**

Works WERE necessary to show faith. Without the work there would have been no justification. This has always been the truth and it still is today. But it is the work of Christ that saves today, not the work of man. In other dispensations the work that was required was a work that men did. In the present dispensation it is a work that Christ has done. This is grace.

This teaching is not something that has been known for only a short time. It is not some doctrine that I have espoused on my on. I was taught it by someone who was taught it by someone else. Songs written long ago declared it: "Jesus paid it all, all to Him I owe. Sin had left a crimson stain, He washed it white as snow."

In past dispensations if a man did not do works he could not be saved. In the present dispensation if man thinks his works saves him he is not saved.

Paul said: **"I do not frustrate the grace of God: for if righteousness come by the law, then Christ is dead in vain."**

Do you want to frustrate the grace of God? Do not allow some false prophet to hoodwink you into believing you must be baptized or speak in tongues to be saved. That would be frustrating the grace of God. That would be a work you could perform, thus frustrating to God and to Christ who did the work required for your salvation.

WHAT WILL IT BE – HEAVEN OR HELL?

Question: If you were to die today, would you spend eternity in heaven or hell?

If you said heaven, praise God and go and share your faith and your assurance with a lost friend, relative, fellow worker or neighbor.

If you said hell or you do not know, read on.

Would you like to know about heaven? If one is to go there they must be saved, they must trust in what Christ has already done for them. How does one come to that point?

1. Recognize you are a sinner: "**For all have sinned and come short of the glory of God.**" Romans 3: 23.

2. Understand the penalty for sin: "**For the wages of sin is DEATH; but the <u>gift of God</u> is eternal life through Jesus Christ our Lord**" Romans 6: 23.

3. Believe the gospel of your salvation: "**Moreover, brethren, I declare unto you the gospel which I preached unto you, which also ye have received, and wherein ye stand; By which also ye are saved, if ye keep in memory what I preached unto you, unless ye have believed in vain. For I delivered unto you first of all that which I also received, how that Christ died for our sins according to the scriptures; And that he was buried, and that he rose again the third day according to the scriptures:**" 1 Corinthians 15: 1-4.

4. Accept the free gift of God: "**For by grace are ye saved through faith; and that not of yourselves: it is the GIFT of God: not of works, lest any man should boast.**" Ephesians 2: 8-9.

Everyone who is alive is a sinner. You are, and so am I. Adam was made in the image of God, but Adam sinned, and everyone who has ever been born is born of fallen Adam. Adam and Eve ate of the tree of the knowledge of good and evil, which was a sin. Everyone that was born of Adam was born in sin and falls short of the glory of God. Since all who are born are born sinners, what we sinners deserve (wages of sin) is death. This death means to be separated from God eternally. But if I accept the gift of God, which is Christ dying for my sins; I will be saved from the wrath of eternal damnation.

God gives us eternal life with Him because of what Christ did on Calvary. And when Christ was resurrected from the grave he conquered death for all who would accept His gift.

Salvation is accepting the gift that has already been provided for you. It is free for you, but it cost God and Christ a lot in order for you to have it. Christ had to die and spend three days and night in hell before God resurrected Him from there.

When Christ died on Calvary over 2,000 years ago, God placed the sins of man, past, present and future, on His shoulders. Jesus Christ redeemed you from your sins. To redeem is to buy back. Until you accept what Christ did, you remain a salve to sin. That sin has separated you from God. Jesus Christ, in redemption, paid the necessary price (His life) and performed the work God required, the shedding of His blood, to restore fallen man's standing with God.

Since you are a sinner, you have all been on "Death Row". The sentence has been handed down by the eternal judge and you have been found lacking. You must die, but you have one last chance to escape eternal death: Accept the gift of Christ. If you do, you will pass from death to life.

ONLY BELIEVE

Most of you reading this will have never met me, but let me speak to you as if I were your closet friend. There is a heaven and there is a hell. When I was a child that was an accepted fact by the majority of the people living in the United States of America, but sadly, it is not the case today.

One day you are going to die. I want you to image that you are in prison and on "Death Row". You're only hope of escaping death would be if someone intervened on your behalf. You've been informed that that someone, Jesus Christ, is coming today. He enters your cell and speaks:

Jesus: "My child, you are in a precarious situation, are you not?"

Doomed Soul: "Yes Sir, I am. Can you help me?"

Jesus: "Yes, I can."

Doomed Soul: "Will you?"

Jesus: "I already have. But up until this point you have refused to accept my gift to you. Will you trust that I have already done what is necessary for you to be free? Will you believe that what I have done will give you a get out of jail free card?"

Doomed Soul: "I would like to believe, but how can I be sure that your word is true?"

Jesus: "Because I just told you. I am the way the truth and the life. The words that I speak are truth. I did everything for you to be free."

Doomed Soul:	"What did you do?"
Jesus:	I died for your transgressions over 2,000 years ago. Men buried me, but my Father raised me from the dead three days later and I ascended back to my Father. Believe I did that for you and you can walk away from here a free person. Nobody will keep you from walking out of here."
Doomed Soul:	"Do you think I'm crazy? Why would you die for me? I've never met you before. There must be something in it for you, so what's the catch? I've always been told you don't get something for nothing."
Jesus:	"I did it because I loved you and I want you to be a part of my family, but you must trust me. Will you?"
Pause	
Jesus:	"Will you trust me? If you will, let's get of here and go home to my Father."
Doomed Soul:	"The minute I walk out of that door those guards will think I'm trying to escape and they will shoot me. You are asking me to put my life in your hands and I do not even know you."

Jesus:	"If you knew me you would trust me. Will you?"
Doomed Soul:	"I want to but I am afraid."
Jesus:	"What is there to be afraid of? You are going to die if you don't trust me, and you're going to live forever in a place of torment eternally. So what have you got to lose? If I walk out of here and you do not follow after me, you will surely die. I am offering you everlasting life in a wonderful place, all you have to do is trust me to be who I say I am. Will you let me save you or not? Believe in me and you will be free."

The man slowly, but a little reluctantly, walks out the cell door and past the guard and out the doors to freedom.

Doomed Soul:	"I believe He meant what He said so I put my life completely in His hands."
Jesus:	"My words are true, you can believe them."
Saved Soul:	"Thank you Lord, for saving my soul and giving me eternal life with you in heaven."

If you are a lost sinner, Christ's words are true and you will find those words in a King James Bible. His Word says believe I died for your sins, was buried and resurrected and you will be saved. Jesus says believe I did that for you and that salvation is by my grace and the work I did on Calvary. Trust my words and salvation is yours. It is God's gift to all who will believe.

BE CAREFUL

There are many people in pulpits who will tell you that you must do this or that in order to be saved. They want you to add something that you can do to the finished work of Christ. The fact is that if you add anything you will loose everything. Jesus Christ redeemed you by the shedding of His blood. **"For by grace are ye saved through faith; and that not of yourselves: it is the gift of God: NOT OF WORKS, lest any man should boast."**

Circumcision never saved anyone. Keeping the Law could not save anyone. Water baptism will not save anyone, nor will doing good works save anyone. Jesus saves! You do not have to walk down an isle and give a preacher your hand; that does not save you. You might cry or you might not, but crying will not save you. Actions and emotions do not aid in your salvation; they may occur, but they do not save.

Jesus paid the price for your salvation. He is all you need. If you add anything to His finished work you prostitute the grace of God. All you can do is trust in what He has already done. You can do that wherever you are: riding in a car, in a motel room, in your home or in the woods. The question is, "Will You?"

If you will, you are saved. Go and serve Him. Find a place that teaches the Bible and begin to grow in the knowledge of Him. **"Study to shew thyself approved unto God, a**

workman that needeth not to be ashamed, rightly dividing the word of truth." 2 Timothy 2: 15.

You can obtain additional information on the ministry of Obed Kirkpatrick by viewing www.soundwordsministry.com.

After Salvation

The Bible: A Christian's Operation Manual

Rules! Rules! Rules!

Everybody at one time or another falls under the various rules of conduct. If you are an American, the Constitution of the United States of America clearly defines specific rights and freedoms of its citizens. The sports world has rules. Your local YMCA has rules. The company one works for has rules. Most of these rules are found in a company's Operation Manual. Although these rules vary from company to company, the purpose of the Operation Manual is to provide a ready source of information. Have a question? Check the Manual.

Christians have a ready source of information to help govern their lives too. It is the Bible. If you have any spiritual questions, check your Bible. My prayer for every Christian: Fall in love with God and His Word. Read your Bible everyday.

Use it as a guide to run your business and your home. If you do, you will have a peace you never dreamed possible.

Some religious denominations have discouraged their members from reading their Bibles. In the 1800's they reprimanded those who did read the Bible on their own, saying it s the responsibility of the priest to interpret the Bible. The Council of Trent actually forbade the reading of the Bible in any language other than Latin. That act in itself restricted many from reading.

Even though God has inspired holy men to write down His words in the scriptures of the Bible, remember God is the author,

"All scripture is given by inspiration of God..." 2 Timothy 3:16.

"Knowing this first, that no prophecy of the scripture if of any PRIVATE INTERPRETATION. For the prophecy came not in old time by the will of man: but by holy men of God spake as they were moved by the Holy Ghost." 2 Peter 1:20-21.

God had men write down the scriptures so that when listening to a Pope, priest, minister, rabbi, we could search the scriptures to see if they were teaching truth.

"These were more noble then those in Thessalonica, in that they received the word with all readiness of mind, and searched the scriptures daily whether those things were so." (Acts 17:11)

Why would a denomination want to discourage the reading of the Bible? It could be that people would find the Bible contradicting denominational issues imposed on them by the mother church. It could be that people would learn they need not fear the Pope, priest, minister, rabbi, they need only fear God.

In recent weeks there has been a lot of media on The Heaven's Gate cult and its leader Charles Applewhite. Thirty nine people committed suicide because they believed what their leader said, rather then believing the Word of God. They saw the Hale-Bopp comet and believed it was a space craft that God had sent for them. So these people killed themselves in order to be transported to the comet and on to heaven. Absurd you say. No, not at all! In the late 1970's hundreds of followers of the late Jim Jones killed themselves. In 1993 the Branch Dividian Cult near Waco, Texas, headed by David Koresh was under siege by the FBI as they feared children were being used by Koresh for sex. The building caught fire and over seventy people died in the flames.

I have often wondered why people would rather place their trust in some charismatic human being rather than simply trusting God. When religious organizations teach there is no possible salvation for anyone who does not sincerely believe what the head of the church teaches, they are nothing more than an occult practice. The heads of religious organizations do not speak for God. God Speaks for Himself through His Word.

God does call preachers/teachers! But God never called a preacher/teacher to usurp His authority or place oneself on the same plane as God. First and foremost, He called preachers/teachers to share the gospel of salvation.

"For whosoever shall call upon the name of the Lord shall be saved. How shall they call on Him in whom they have

not believed? And how shall they believe in Him whom they have not heard? And how shall they hear without a preacher?" Romans 10:13-14.

Preachers and teachers alike are servants of God, not equal with God. God has no equal! God has never chosen or appointed any man to act as His equal. The apostles and prophets of old were only a voice for God. The Bible has always been the final authority of the mind of God. Use it, read it, study it, for in it alone will you find supreme comfort.

The Bible has sixty-six books. The printed Bibles of today have been divided by man into two divisions: Old Testament with 39 books and New Testament with 27 books. Within these two divisions we find certain distinctive divisions which, in theological circles, are called dispensations. (Greek-*oikonomia*)

Strong's Concordance defines *oikonomia* as: administration (of a household or estate); specifically a (religious) "economy"; dispensation, stewardship. *Oikonomia* comes from the Greek work, *oikonomos*, defined as: a house-distributor (i.e. manager) or overseer, i.e. an employee in that capacity: by extension. A fiscal agent (treasurer); fig. a preacher (of the gospel): chamberlain, governor, steward.

For the purpose of this writing, I wish to use the definition: management of a household to emphasize my point. When managing our earthly households, we make budgetary changes from time to time.

Example: A young married couple establishes a budget when they first get married. They allocate $150.00 a month for groceries. Plenty, they say for two people. As the years go by the family gets larger; prices go up, and the size of the family doubles. So, there is a need to do away with the old budgeted amount for food and establish a new one, say $300.00 a month. Ten years out and this need to make changes will once again become a necessity. So, we make necessary adjustments: add to, subtract from, or do away with and start all over.

God has managed His people throughout the Bible in just the same way. When Adam was created, he was created innocent of sin. God dealt with or dispensed instructions to Adam in a state of innocence. Then Adam sinned. With the conscience awareness of sin, God had to deal with him differently than He did in innocence. Many theologians have listed the first three dispensations as Innocence, Conscience, and Human Government, the third coming about when man was given the responsibility to govern the world for God.

When God called Abraham, He made a promise to bless him and his seed. So the Dispensation of Promise is suggested as being the next dispensation. There are numerous scriptures that mention the promises of God to Abraham and the passing on of those promises through Isaac and Jacob.

Then along came Moses and a need for a new dispensation: The Dispensation of the Law. The law was given specifically to Israel. It consisted of not only the Ten Commandments but some six hundred plus laws found in the Book of Leviticus.

In Ephesians 3: 1-2 we read of another dispensation: The Dispensation of the Grace of God.

"For this cause I Paul, the prisoner of Jesus Christ for you Gentiles, if ye have heard of the dispensation of the grace of God which is given me to you-ward:".

It is in this dispensation, the dispensation of the grace of God, we of the 21st Century live. And if you study your Bible, you will find that this dispensation of the grace of God, given to Paul and specifically given to Gentiles, contains information and instructions to be followed today unlike any given in past dispensations. Many of the things found in the Pauline Epistles (Romans through Philemon) you cannot find anywhere else in your Bible.

If God has changed the way He deals with His people in the past, and He has: and if Paul in the above scripture tells of a new dispensations given to him specifically for Gentiles, it would behoove each of us to diligently find out what this new dispensation is all about. Let me hasten to say that all scripture has a purpose and all scripture is for us, Old and New Testament alike.

"All scripture is given by inspiration of God, and is profitable for doctrine, for reproof, for correction, for instruction in righteousness: That the man of God may be perfect, thoroughly furnished unto all good works." 2 Timothy 3: 16-17.

But if one is a good student of the scripture, one must not overlook another passage found in 2 Timothy: **"Study to shew thyself approved unto God, a workman that needeth not to be ashamed, rightly dividing the Word of Truth."** 2 Timothy 2:15.

We believe that every book in the Bible is FOR us. But we also believe that the Pauline Epistles are exclusively TO us. Example: In the Old Testament, an animal sacrifice was to be made as an offering for the remission of sin.

In the dispensation of the grace of God we know that the blood of Jesus Christ is the only sacrifice we need. There is no longer a need to offer up animals as had once been required. The animal sacrifice has been done away with. Even though you can read about it in your Bible where an animal sacrifice was required, it does not apply TO us today.

The mailman delivers our personal mail along with a lot of mail addressed to occupant. It is the personal mail that is meaningful, often times uplifting, sometimes bringing bad news. Nonetheless, it is mail intended for you and I individually. The Pauline Epistles are representative of our personal mail. These epistles were written directly to the Church the Body of Christ and are to be followed even though they say things which seemingly contradict other scripture

Let me be very clear. The Bible does not contradict itself! Those who say it does are being used of the devil to get you to swallow that "hog wash" and keep you from enjoying what God has for you. Do not fall into the trap of getting spiritual answers from men, preachers, and non-preachers. Listen to them, but then check their words with the words of the Bible. If there is contradictory information, men are always at fault. God's word is true! Remember, it is not what one thinks the scripture says it is what the scriptures say that matters. Start your Christian walk depending on the God of Truth, not the man of God.

If you were given this booklet to read after you trusted Christ as your Savior, let me be very clear about something. The moment you became a child of God the Holy Spirit came into your body. You and Christ are one and the Spirit that now dwells inside you will reveal truth unto you.

"But as it is written, eye hath not seen, nor ear heard, neither have entered into the heart of man, the things which God hath prepared for them that love Him. But God hath revealed them unto us by His Spirit: for the Spirit searcheth all things, yea, the deep things of God. For what man knoweth the things of a man, save the spirit of man which is in him? Even so the things of God knoweth no man, but the Spirit of God. Now we have received, not the spirit of the world, but the Spirit which is of God; that we might know the things that are freely given to us of God." 1 Corinthians 2:9-12

If you are saved, learn to depend upon the Word of God. Get into a regular habit of study. Reading is good but study is better. Remember, man will let you down; God will never disappoint you nor confuse you. Only man will do those things. While there are many pastors, priests, and rabbis who may have been a source of blessing for us all, man is still man and is subject to err. If your total trust is in man and man alone you are subject to become puppets, manipulated into doing anything, even committing suicide. Sooner or later man will be the source of disillusionment. Do not despair and turn away from God, but run to Him and away from man as quickly as your legs will carry you.

As you start your Christian walk, start by depending upon God and His Word. He has made sure you have a Bible in your own language to read and study. The Bible is the Christian's Operation Manual. A church creed or code of ethics should never be placed with equal authority along side the Word of God.

The Bible gives us comfort when we are comfortless; strength when we are weak; joy in the midst of sorrow; hope for the future and it lifts us up when we are down. God never said that once you are saved that everything would be "a bed of roses." What He did say was: "**Let your conversation be without covetousness and be content with such things as ye have; for He hath said, I will never leave thee, nor forsake thee.**" Hebrews 13:5

Rest assured God is never the One that leaves. Man strays from God, not God from man. Learning to trust completely in Him will lead to eternal happiness, even in the midst of sorrow. There is a light at the end of the darkness. Patiently wait! It will come.

Salvation/Regeneration

We have learned that we are living in the dispensation of the Grace of God. So we are going to focus on how we are saved in this dispensation. Remember, God in dispensations past may have required certain things (animal sacrifices) but later on decided to abolish those things. We are not going to concern ourselves with past dispensations and their requirements for salvation. We will focus on the subject at hand for this present day dispensation. Let us look at two passages of scripture.

"**For by grace are you saved through faith; and that not of yourselves; it is the gift of God; not of works, lest any man should boast.**" Ephesians 2:8-9

"**Moreover, brethren, I declare unto you the gospel which I preached unto you, which ye have also received, and wherein ye stand; by which also ye are saved, if you keep in memory what I preached unto you, unless ye have believed in vain. For I delivered unto you first of all that which I also received, how that Christ died for our sins according to the scripture and the He was buried and**

that He rose again on the third day according to the scriptures." 1 Corinthians 15:1-4

In a nutshell, what do these scriptures tell us?

1. We are saved by grace. (Even though we do not deserve it, God gave His only begotten Son to die for us.
2. Salvation is a gift. (a gift is something someone else gives, most of the time it is because they care for you)
3. Salvation is not of works. (Work is doing something and expecting something in return. It is getting paid for a job well done)
4. The gospel saves. (The word gospel is often defined as "good news." So what is the "good news?" that saves?)
5. The gospel is: Christ died for our sins, was buried and rose again the third day.

In this dispensation of the gospel of the grace of God, man is saved believing that Christ, the Son of God, died on the cross of Calvary for man's sin. If He had to die so that man could be saved from sin, we must conclude that all men are sinners and in need of a Savior.

Remember. We said that one must not take what man says without having scripture to back up his words, right? So what does God's Word say about the subject? **"For all have sinned and come short of the glory of God."** Romans 3:23

Scripture clearly tells us that all men are sinners and all men fall short of what God requires for entrance into the family of God. Sin stands in the way between man and God. **"For**

the wages of sin is death; but the gift of God is eternal life through Jesus Christ our Lord." Romans 6:23

1. "Wages if Sin" This implies there is some payment one should get for being a sinner. We already know from Romans 3:23 that we are all sinners, right? That all definitely includes you and me and everyone else in the whole wide world.

2. "Wages of Sin is Death." Now I know that because I am a sinner I should make a payment for sin. According to the passage, the only payment God will accept is Death. Why? Sin is an act of rebellion against God's demand for holiness, and payment for that rebellion is death.

3. "But the gift of God"....What was the gift of God? Jesus Christ! Christ died on the cross for all men so that they might be saved. What a precious gift. What a wonderful faith Jesus had.

4, "Is eternal life through Jesus Christ our Lord." If I believe that Christ had enough faith in God to raise Him from the dead so that He could give this gift of eternal life to man, I am saved-for eternity. And it is not because of anything I did, but because of what He did. Christ died for my sins. I trust in His saving grace and I get to live forever with Him in heaven.

God is just. If we are to stand before God in eternity we must be made just, or be justified. Jesus did that for us also. Look what the scriptures have to say about that. "**Knowing that a man is not justified by the works of the law but by the Faith OF Christ, even we have believed IN Jesus Christ, that we might be justified by the Faith OF Christ, and**

not by the works of the law: for by the works of the law shall no flesh be justified." Galatians 2:16

We have eternal life through Jesus Christ because He (Christ) had faith that God would not leave His soul in hell and would raise him from the grave. "**For thou will not leave my soul in hell; neither will thou suffer thine Holy One to see corruption.**" Psalm 16:10

If we believe that Christ died for our sins, was buried, and rose again the third day, we are saved. We are justified. Not because of our faith, but because of HIS faith we are saved. (I detailed this in my book: Faith of Christ).

The Scripture says that when Jesus died, we died. "**I am crucified with Christ; nevertheless I live; yet not I, but Christ liveth in me; and the life I now live in the flesh I live by the faith OF the Son of God. Who loved me and gave Himself for me.**" Galatians 2;20

How can someone be crucified and yet live? Christ, who lives in me, died in my place. There is a song that says "He paid a debt He did not owe," for He was not a sinner, as the song continues it states, "I owed a debt I could not pay." I could not die for my sin or offer an animal sacrifice that would please God. Jesus Christ paid the price for my sin. He died on the cross. He alone met God's requirement for settling the sin issue.

"**That if thou shalt confess with thy mouth the Lord Jesus and shalt believe in thine heart that God hath raised Him from the dead, thou shalt be saved.**" Romans 10:9

"**For whosoever shall call upon the name of the Lord shall be saved.**" Romans 10:13

You will not find one verse of scripture that says you have to walk down an isle to be saved. Nor will you find any passage of scripture that says you must pray through until you receive the victory in order to be saved. I have been unable to find one place in the Pauline Epistles, our authority in the dispensation of the grace of God that says you have to be sorry for your sins if you are to be saved. Yet there are fundamental churches across the world that tells their members these things are necessary. Don't believe them.

There are too many churches today that play upon your emotions. But emotions have nothing to do with your salvation or your regeneration. Does that mean you will not get emotional once you see the real truth about salvation? Not at all! You may cry or you might shout for joy. But then again, you may not do either. Whether you get emotional or do not get emotional does not determine whether or not you are saved. The determining factor for salvation is what Christ did for you and your believing it, trusting in it completely. Jesus paid it all. All to him I owe. Sin had left a crimson stain. He washed it white as snow. What great words from a wonderful song.

What is salvation? It is a free gift of God. That gift was Jesus Christ. He died as a sacrifice for sin. He took that sin into the grave and left it there when He rose the third day. Because of His resurrection, we have power over death and hell. We also have eternal life because we have become part of Christ's body. We become a part of Him and He becomes a part of us. In the book of Ephesians we are told about the quickening, the raising up, and the seating together of Christ.

"Even when we were dead in sin, hath He quickened us together with Christ. (By grace ye are saved;) and hath

raised us up together, and made us sit together in heavenly places in Christ Jesus. Ephesians 2:5,6

There are other passages of Scriptures that talk about "to quicken", or "make alive", but only here and Colossians 2:13 do we find the words "with Him". It is a teaching that is exclusive to the teaching of the "Mystery."

It is amazing that there are seven (the number of perfection) associations the believer has with Christ in this Age of Grace. These seven associations :

1. The Cross: We are crucified with Christ
2. The Death: We are dead with Christ
3. The Burial We are buried with Christ
4. The Present Salvation Experience: We are quickened with Christ
5. The Resurrection: We are raised with Christ
6. The Ascension: We are seated with Christ
7. The Glory: We are manifested with Christ

Christ died. We died. Christ was buried. We are buried. Christ was raised from the dead. We are raised from the dead. Christ ascended and is seated at the right hand of the Father. We are to be resurrected and seated at the right hand of the Father. Christ is glorified with the Father. We are glorified with the Father.

I settled the issue of my salvation over 50 years ago. Do you remember having done so? If you did, you have eternal life with God in heaven. If you didn't you have eternal life, but with Satan in hell. Salvation is a gift. Have you received it? If you haven't, will you? Right now- trust in the saving grace of Jesus Christ.

Chapter Three

Eternal Security

Can you know you are saved? Can you have complete assurance that you will live with God in eternity when you die? Yes, you can!!! But let me hasten to say, not all religions believe that. Why? They built a religious organization based upon man's interpretation of the Scripture. They do not rightly divide the Scriptures. They do not believe that the church the body of Christ is any different than the church in the wilderness. They believe we are still under the law today and not under Grace. They believe works, being good, going to church regularly saves, and on and on and on.

Paul, the apostle of grace warned the Galatians of a false gospel: "**I marvel that ye are so soon removed** (Greek: *metecho* - turned away, deserting from) **from him that called you into the grace of Christ unto another** (Greek *heteros* - different or altered) **gospel. Which is not another** (Greek: *allos* - of the same kind) **but there be some that trouble you** (Greek: *tarasso*- disturb or agitate) **you, and would pervert the gospel of Christ. But though we, or an angel from heaven, preach any other gospel unto you than that which We have preached unto you, let him be accursed. As we have said before, so say I now again, if any man preach any other gospel unto you than that you have received, let him be accursed." Galatians 1:6-9

Paul, the Apostle of Grace, preached grace to those of Galatia. After his departure from the area others came who preached a different gospel than Paul had preached. Paul was more than a little upset that these folks had removed themselves from his teaching, the teaching which led to their salvation, and were following after another whose teaching was not after grace. Paul was emphatic when he stated there was but one gospel, and the correct one was the one he had preached unto them.

Fact: If we do not believe that Christ did everything necessary for our salvation, we will not believe we have eternal security. Herein lays the problem with those who "hope they go to heaven when they die."

Religions that add works as a part of salvation/ regeneration: baptism, speaking in tongues, etc. must base their hope of eternal life on works or being in a state of goodness when they die. They live constantly in fear, always hoping that God will forgive them for any sins they have committed once they were saved. They do not believe what their Bible says.

"And you being dead in your sins and the uncircumcision of your flesh, hath He quickened together with Him, HAVING FORGIVEN YOU ALL TRESPASSES." Colossians 2;13

Let's look at the above passage of scripture carefully:

1. **"You being dead in your sins"** To better understand these words, we need to look at several other passages of scripture. **"Know ye not, that as many of us as were baptized into Jesus Christ were baptized into His death."** Romans 6:3 **"Now if we be dead with Christ, we believe that we shall also live with Him."** Romans 6:8

   How is one baptized into the death of Christ? By sprinkling water over one's head? By dunking someone in a baptismal pool? I think not! The Bible says: **"For by one Spirit are we all baptized into one body"**.....1 Corinthians 12:13

   "For as many of you as have been baptized into Christ have put on Christ." Galatians 3:27

   Baptism into Jesus Christ is a work of the Holy Spirit. It is a spiritual baptism, not a physical one. Baptism with water does not do anything but get one wet. We are dead in our sins or dead to sin because of the relationship we have with Jesus Christ after we have trusted Him.

   " Now if we be dead with Christ, we believe that we shall also live with Him: knowing that Christ being raised from the dead dieth no more; death hath no more dominion over Him, for in that He died, he died unto sin once: but in that He liveth, He liveth unto God, likewise reckon yourself to be dead indeed unto sin, but alive unto God through Jesus Christ our Lord." Romans 6:8-11

We are dead to sin because Christ died for our sins. Death has no dominion over the saved, just as it had no dominion over Christ.

2. **"Quickened together with Him."** When we accept what Jesus did for us we died with Him, we were buried with Him and we were resurrected with Him. We are part pf Jesus Christ and He is part of us. Where He is, we are. The very fact that we are part of His body assures us of a position in heaven, where Jesus is seated at the right hand of the Father. Look and see for yourself, then believe:

"But God, who is rich in mercy, for His great love wherewith He loved us, even when we were dead in sins, hath quickened us together WITH CHRIST, (By Grace ye are saved) and hath raised us up together and made us sit together in heavenly places in Christ Jesus." Ephesians 2:4-6

"That we should be to the praise of His glory who first trusted in Christ. In whom ye also trusted, after that ye heard the work of truth, the gospel of your salvation: in whom also after that ye believed ye WERE SEALED with that Holy Spirit of promise. " Ephesians 1:12-13

God not only promised us a heavenly position, He placed a seal on us to guarantee our getting there. We are sealed by the Holy Spirit of God. Nothing we do can undo that sealing. We are assured the sealing will be good until Christ redeems us from this present world. **"And grieve not the Holy Spirit of God, whereby ye are sealed unto the day of redemption."** Ephesians 4:30

3. **"Having forgiven you all trespasses."** Having forgiven is past tense, indicating our sins were taken care of in a prior time period. When was it? It was some 2000 years ago at Calvary that the price for sin was paid. Sins were taken care of with the shedding of the blood of Jesus Christ. If I worry as to whether or not my sins will be forgiven I do not believe the death of Christ was sufficient. It stands to reason if Christ's death was sufficient enough to save me, it is sufficient enough to sustain me.

   Christ died for sin one time and that one time was good enough to last throughout all time. If you fear separation from God every time you sin, you are saying the death of Jesus Christ had no lasting effect, making it necessary for Him to die over and over again each and every time anyone sins. How ridiculous to think that!! How can anyone swallow that kind of garbage? Yet many do.

When Jesus offered up His body for the sins of man, He sat down with God. He could not have sat down if the work He came to do had not been completed. Look for yourself!

"By the which will we are sanctified through the offering of the body of Jesus Christ ONCE FOR ALL.....but this man, after He had offered ONE SACRIFICE for sins FOREVER, SAT DOWN ON THE RIGHT HAND OF God....for my ONE OFFERING he hath perfected FOREVER them that are sanctified." Hebrews 10: 10,11,12.

Christ paid the price for the barrier that separated man from God- Sin. If you fully understand that, then you cannot but conclude that eternal life is part of the gift God gave us in

Christ. There are so many passages of scripture that speak of eternal life, but we will only quote two.

"**Who shall separate us from the love of Christ? Shall tribulation, or distress, or persecution, or famine, or nakedness, or peril, or sword? As it is written, For thy sake we are killed all the day long; we are accounted as sheep for the slaughter. Nay, in all these things we are more than conquerors through Him that loved us. For I am persuaded, that neither death, nor life, nor angels, nor principalities, nor powers, nor things present, nor things to come, nor height nor depth, nor any other creature, shall be able to separate us from the love of God, which is in Christ Jesus our Lord.**" Romans 8:35-39

What can we be sure of?

1. Christ died for our sins some 2000 years ago.
2. His death was for all sin of all people, past, present and future.
3. He only had to die once.
4. We are already spiritually seated in heavenly places, so how is it possible to not go to heaven? It isn't.
5. Christ is in me. Because He is, I have a hop of eternal life. "…**which is Christ in you the hope of glory.**" Colossians 1:27

That hope is to be with Him in Glory. This is not " I hope I will get there." This is a positive statement. Since Christ is in us, and He is if we have trusted him as our Savior. We have a promised hope of being in glory with him.

6. Nothing can separate us from the love of God which is in Christ Jesus our Lord.

Who had eternal security? All who have accepted the finished work of Christ. Christ
Died for our sins, was buried , and rose again the third day, ascended up into heaven and
Is seated at the right hand of the Father.

Can you lose your salvation in the Age of Grace? No! No! No! A thousand times, no! **"For ye are dead, and your life is hid with Christ in God. When Christ, who is our life, shall appear, then shall ye also appear with Him in glory."** Colossians 3:3-4.

Now, are there any more questions? If there are, you have either not believed the Scriptures listed above, or are lost, or you need someone to go a little slower.

BAPTISM

In all my 30 plus years in the ministry, I know of no other single subject that has been the center of so many arguments and bitterness as the subject of baptism. It places men into separate camps and creates divisions you would never have imagined. Many years ago Mr. J.N. Darby was asked what he held as to baptism. He said, "I hold my tongue." But we need not do that today. Nay! We must not for it is too important.

I was brought up in a Southern Baptist Church and for years fully supported the practices of that faith. After many years of study I came to understand the truth of rightly dividing as revealed through the teaching of the Apostle Paul. When I learned of the "mystery hid in God," I also learned of the one baptism associated with the mystery, which is spiritual and is completely different from the baptism of John.

There are verses in the Bible that state baptism is necessary for the remission of sins. Peter and the eleven were commissioned to go into the world, baptizing in the name of the Father, Son and Holy Ghost. But in another passage of scripture they are told to baptize in the name of Jesus Christ.

"Go ye therefore, and teach all nations, baptizing them in the name of the Father, and of the Son, and of the Holy Ghost: Teaching them to observe all things whatsoever I have commanded you. and, lo, I am with you always, even unto the end of the world. Amen." Matthew 28: 19-20

"Then Peter said unto them, Repent, and be baptized every one of you in the name of Jesus Christ for the remission of sins, and ye shall receive the gift of the Holy Ghost." Acts 2:38

To emphasize just how divisive the subject of baptism is, let us look at just one point: how to baptize. One group of believers baptizes in the name of the Father, Son, and Holy Ghost. Another baptizes in the name of Jesus Christ. Both believe the others to be wrong. And so the arguments begin. See what I mean?

The traditional view of water baptism is that baptism is an ordinance of the denomination and is to be observed by all members of The Body of Christ. John Calvin has stated "that baptism is to us the seal of salvation which Christ obtained for us." But I have a problem with water baptism being the baptism of importance for today. Indeed, I have a problem with water baptism being necessary at all. Why? If Paul is the apostle to the Gentiles, and he is; then why would he say, **"Christ sent me NOT to baptize"** in 1 Corinthians 1:17 if water baptism is so important.

Having made the above statement, I have already placed a wedge between me and those who do believe that water baptism is included in God's plan for this dispensation. I wish this weren't true. But it is. I stand on the scripture. "**There is ONE BODY and ONE SPIRIT, even as ye are called in ONE HOPE of your calling. ONE LORD, ONE FAITH, ONE BAPTISM, ONE GOD and FATHER of all, who is above all, and through all, and in you all.**" Ephesians 4:4-6.

That ONE BAPTISM is spiritual, not physical. The question is not whether water baptism is found in the scriptures, it is. John came preaching water baptism. He baptized Jesus and Jesus instructed his disciples to baptize, as we have already seen. But the questions that need to be answered: 1) Is water baptism for us in the dispensation of the grace of God? 2) Should it be administered or practiced today?

Ask any fundamental preacher today to define the gospel of salvation! Will they say, "repent and be baptized for the remission of sins?" or "Christ died for our sins?" Is there any difference in those two statements? Yes, there is. Which statement bears true to the dispensation of the grace of God? Answer: Christ died for our sins!

What affects the way one thinks about baptism is the view that an individual takes concerning the beginning of the Church the Body of Christ. Did it begin with Peter at Pentecost in Acts two or did it in fact begin with Paul and the revelation of the Mystery?

If your preacher believes that the Church the Body of Christ began with the outpouring of the Spirit on the day of Pentecost in Acts two, he must also believe what Peter preached on that day. Peter did not preach that Christ died for their sins. He preached, **"repent and be baptized every one of you in the name of Jesus Christ for the remission of sins."** Acts 2:38

Most fundamentalist who hold to the Acts two position for the beginning of the Body of Christ have learned to waltz around the true meaning of the scripture. For instance, when you ask them to explain Mark 16:16 **"He that believeth and is baptized shall be saved but he that believeth no shall be dammed."**

They have one of two answers:

1. The passages from verse nine to the end of Mark 16 are not found in the two most ancient manuscripts.
2. Or they will say the passage really says, "He that believeth and is saved should then be immersed in believer's baptism."

We can eliminate the first objection by simply showing the other passages of scripture emphasizing repent and be baptized for the remission of sins that are in the older manuscripts: Matthew 28: 19-20; Mark 1:4, Acts 2:38.

John's baptism was a " **baptism of repentance for the remission of sins."** Mark 3:3

Question? Why did Jesus come to John **"to be baptized of him?"** Matthew 3:13.

Did Jesus have sins that needed to be confessed? I think not. God's Word says otherwise: **"For He hath made him to be sin for us, who knew no sin."** 2 Corinthians 5:21

But when John, who knew that the Messiah should be the one to baptize him said, "**I need to be baptized of thee.**" Matthew 3:14 What did Jesus say? "**And Jesus answering said unto him, suffer it to be so now, for thus it becometh us to fulfill all righteousness. Thus he suffered Him.**" Matthew 3:15

Jesus came to be the sacrificial Lamb of God and was baptized to fulfill all righteousness of the law. Jesus was not guilty of sin, even though He eventually goes to Calvary and dies for the sins of men.

The one baptism of Ephesians 4:5 is the same baptism of Romans 6:3-4 and Galatians 3:27. "**Know ye not, that so many of us as were baptized into Jesus Christ were baptized into His death? Therefore we are buried with Him by baptism into death: that like as Christ was raised up from the dead by the glory of the Father, even so we also should walk in newness of life.**" Romans 5:3-4 "**For as many of you as have been baptized into Christ have put on Christ.**" Galatians 3:27

Those who attempt to put water in these passages of scriptures must believe that water baptism is essential to salvation and should receive it before the believer can become a member of the Body of Christ. The baptism in all of the above passages is not water, it is spiritual. You are alive, yes? Then how can you be baptized into Christ's death unless it is spiritual? You can't! It can only be accomplished by a spiritual baptism.

There is not one true grace preacher today that will say water baptism is required for salvation. Most of them are dogmatic in their belief that we are saved by grace through the faith of Christ. Baptism may make one a member of a particular religious organization, but it does not make one a member of the Church the Body of Christ. Which membership is more important? Which membership guarantees eternal life? Then of which membership should you want to be a part?

It would be very difficult for a religious organization that has been in existence for many years to one day stand up and admit their doctrinal statement on baptism was wrong. It would be wonderful if they would do that, but I do not think I will live long enough to see it happen. So what choice do they have but to say something like, "what that really means is once you are saved you should follow Christ in believer's baptism."

What should they say? "I have discovered the meaning of the mystery that Paul preaches and recognized that the practice of water baptism is not for the Church the Body of Christ today." To adhere to tradition, in deference to the Word of God is to lead people into confusion. Guess what? God is NOT the author of confusion, the devil is. " **God is not the author of confusion, but of peace, as in all churches of the saints.**" 1 Corinthians 14:33

So our adversary, the devil, is up to his subtle trickery trying to divide believers. Satan uses all kinds of devious methods to rob believers of true spirituality and a fulfilling life with Christ. Don't allow him to do it to you. The test of a true believer is to check the scriptures to see if the minister, priests, rabbi, evangelist, denomination or whatever is telling you what the Word of God says. **"These were more noble than those in Thessalonica, in that they received the Word with all readiness of mind and searched the scriptures daily, whether those things were so."** Acts:17:11.

LIVING IN A SYSTEM

Once when I was chairman of the Deacons at one of the fastest growing Southern Baptist Churches in central Louisiana, a saved Methodist friend who had been attending our services regularly, inquired about membership in our church. The pastor, whom I loved and dearly love even today, said, " We would love to have you as a member. Have you been baptized in a Baptist Church since you believed?" The answer from this friend was, "no!" "However, I have been baptized in a Methodist Church." To which the pastor replied, "it is a doctrine of our church that you must be baptized of like faith (Baptist) and order (Southern Baptist) if you are to be a member of our fellowship."

This person never joined our church. Feeling that Baptism was nothing more than a church ritual, he saw no need to be re-baptized. He was right! Baptism only made one a member of that church. It had nothing to do with one's spirituality or one's membership in the Church the Body of Christ.

My sister and younger brother had been subtly giving me grace reading material for birthdays and Christmas gifts. I read them and agreed with most of the things about salvation by grace, eternal security, etc. But I had a problem believing that water baptism was not part of God's program for today. But the incident with the Methodist friend challenged me to prove once and for all the necessity for, or the elimination of, baptism.

I spent months studying. Every piece of literature I found on the subject challenged me to dig deeper. I read material written by the Methodist, Baptist, Presbyterian and Church of Christ. The more I read, the more confused I became. The more confused I became, the madder I got. "Can't any of these denominations agree on the issue of baptism," I said.

Then I finally realized that water baptism was not important in this Age of Grace. My brother and sister had tried to tell me that for months. They had been right, but I hated to admit they were. I was a deacon, a Sunday school teacher for ten plus years. How could I not have known that before now? Answer: I had allowed myself to become enamored with my denomination rather than the Word of God.

My intense study made me realize how little I really knew about the Bible. The more I studied, the more I realized I had not been fed adequately on the important things of God's Word. The longer I stayed in my church, the more disappointed I became. I needed more meat. I was tired of being fed milk.

OUT OF BONDAGE AND INTO FREEDOM

As I reflect back to my years of being in denominational churches, I have realized I had been a bond slave to a religion. There were too many "don't do this and don't do that" kinds of sermons, rather than on positive things of God. There were constant prodding's to get more involved in the activities of the church: choir, visitation, bus ministry, deacon meetings, committee on committee meetings, finance meetings, church softball and on and on it went. There was too little emphasis on getting to know more about who we are in Christ, what we have in Christ and what is right for today.

The more I studied the more zeal I had to tell the world about the freedom we have in Christ. I had discovered the Bible is easy to understand if you but know who you are in Christ and in what dispensation you are living. God had challenged me on the one issue of baptism, but in doing so, He had opened my eyes to so much more: the distinctiveness of Pauline doctrine, the mystery, the dispensation of the grace of God and how to rightly divide the Word of truth.

I had been in a system that spoke of liberty in Christ Jesus, but in practice placed you under the bondage of the law; a system that spoke of salvation by grace, but stated the need for works: to be baptized in water; that said the church places few restrictions on what you say or do, but condemned you if what you said or did was not in complete agreement with the governing body of deacons or the Southern Baptist Convention.

I left my church and began having Bible classes in my home. Friends and neighbors came, listened and learned. God blesses His word. For the first time in years I felt free. Without knowing it, I had been in bondage to the law, but now I knew the truth. Dear friend, " **the truth will make you free**." John 8:32

Facts:

1. Peter was commissioned by Jesus Christ to preach the baptism of repentance for the remission of sins.
2. Paul said: He was not sent to baptize.
3. If Peter did not preach the necessity of water baptism he would have been an unfaithful servant to our Lord.
4. If Paul did preach the necessity of water baptism he would have been an unfaithful servant of our Lord.
5. The baptism of John (water) was a part of the dispensation of the law.

6. The one baptism (spiritual) of Ephesians 4 is a part of the dispensation of the Grace of God.
7. Water baptism does not make one a member of the Church of the Body of Christ, spiritual baptism does.

We are living in the Age of Grace and are no longer under the law. **"And if by grace: then it is no more of works: otherwise grace is no more grace."** Romans 11:6

Even though the word baptism does not appear in the Old Testament does not mean the ordinance did not exist. The Jewish religion had many baptisms. **"Which stood only in meats and drinks, and divers washings, and carnal ordinances imposed on them until the time of reformation."** Hebrews 9:10

The Greek work for washings is *baptismo* and is derived from two other Greek words: *bapto* and *baptizo*. The meaning is to wash or cover with fluid. The priests would wash every sacrificial animal as well as their hands. It was symbolic of cleansing. It was also ceremonial. We find it mentioned in Exodus 12:22 and Leviticus 4:6-17 where it refers to the priest dipping his finger or hyssop in blood. In Numbers 19: 18-19 it is used in a ceremony to make something clean which had otherwise been considered unclean. In Hebrews 6:1 2 baptism is referred to as elementary and something they should stop doing. **"Therefore leaving the principles of the doctrine of Christ, let us go on unto perfection, not laying again the foundation of repentance from dead works, and of faith toward God, of the doctrine of baptisms, and of laying on of hands, and of resurrection of the dead, and of eternal judgment."**

If you check the Scriptures you will see baptism was an integral part of the Jewish religion. That is why the Pharisees never asked John the meaning of baptism. All they wanted to know was why he was performing the ritual if he were neither Christ or Elijah the prophet. **"And they asked him, and said unto him, Why baptizeth thou then if thou be not that Christ, nor Elias, neither that prophet?"** John 1:25

This baptism of John was not some new ceremony he had devised. It had been a practice of the Jewish religion long before John the Baptist was ever born. Baptism was a command. It was essential to cleansing and forgiveness of sins. It was an act of purification and that subject became a matter of dispute. **"Then there arose a question between some of John's disciples and the Jews about purifying."** John 3: 25

During the time baptism was being performed, it was a part of the law and a direct command from the Lord. **"Go ye therefore and teach all nations, baptizing them in the name of the Father, and of the Son, and of the Holy Ghost."** Matthew 28:19

Baptism was not an arbitrary thing before the ministry of Christ or during His ministry. It had to be done or you would be in violation of the command of God. But that no longer is true.

Christ shed His blood and He nailed the ordinances of the past to the tree on which he died. **"Blotting out the handwriting of ordinances that was against us, which was contrary to us, and took it out of the way, nailing it to His cross."** (Colossians 2:14) Water baptism is not in God's program for today.

Tongues, Healings, and Signs

Speaking in tongues, public healing meetings and looking for "signs and wonders" is sweeping the world at an alarming rate. Are these things for us today? Many think so. But I for one do not. I believe that millions of sincere Christians are being deceived by Satan on these issues thus frustrating the grace of God.

It all comes down to this one issue: people not knowing the difference between the gospel committed to Peter and the gospel committed unto Paul. **"But contrariwise, when they saw the gospel of the uncircumcision was committed unto me, as the gospel of the circumcision was unto Peter: and when James, Cephas, and John, who seemed to be pillars, perceived the grace that was given unto me, they gave to me and Barnabas the right hands of fellowship; that we should to unto the heathen, and they to the circumcision."** Galatians 2: 7-9

I believe that were it not for the ministers of grace preaching the gospel of the grace of God, Satan would deceive the whole world.

"And the great dragon was cast out, that old serpent called the Devil and Satan, which deceiveth the whole world..." Revelation 12:9

Ministers who persist on taking one back to Pentecost for the beginning of the dispensation of grace have taken Christian minds off the goals and objectives of the Pauline books of Ephesians, Philippians and Colossians.

We are always hearing the works "Back to Pentecost" from full gospel fellowships. And I say, "What for?" What sound minded individual would want to go back under the bondage of the law? Not I! I hope I have matured enough to know when I am being given information not intended for me today. We are warned by Paul of just that. "**That we henceforth be no more children, tossed to and fro, and carried about by every wind of doctrine, by the sleight of men, and cunning craftiness, wherby they lie in wait to deceive.**" Ephesians 4:14

Mark 16: 15-18 is invariably used by ministers of the signs movement. Let us look at what it says. "**And He said unto them, go ye into all the world, and preach the gospel to every creature. He that believeth and is baptized shall be saved; but he that believeth not shall be dammed. And these signs shall follow them that believe; In my name they shall cast out devils; they shall speak with new tongues; they shall take up serpents; and if they drink any deadly thing it shall not hurt them; they shall lay hands on the sick, and they shall recover.**"

TAKE WHAT YOU WANT, LEAVE OUT WHAT YOU DON'T WANT

Upon examining Mark 16, this is what we find:

1. If you believe and are baptized you shall be saved.
2. If you do not believe, you shall be damned.
3. Those who believe shall be able to do all of the things that follow:
   A. SHALL cast out devils
   B. SHALL speak with new tongues
   C. SHALL take up serpents
   D. SHALL drink any deadly thing without it hurting them

  E. SHALL lay hands on the sick and
  F. They SHALL recover.

Question? What does the word "shall" mean?

  Does it mean maybe?
  Does it mean ought to?
  Does it mean if you have enough faith?

The word shall carries the meaning of inevitability, determination, or promise.

It is very clear that if you were a believer, you would be capable of performing all those things listed in the passage. But that is not what is being taught. Only some people heal, some cast out devils and a few take up serpents. But the verses specifically say all believers shall be capable of performing all the things listed.

The verses DO NOT SAY: "A few will be able to do one thing and another few will be able to do another thing."

Nor do the verses say: "Pick out a few signs that fit your personality and let them be for you."

There is one more thing that makes me question so called faith healers. When you pin them down as to why one particular person was not healed after the laying on of their hands, they usually always reply "They did not have enough faith to believe they would be healed."

Show me one passage of scripture that said faith was a prerequisite to healing. For that matter, show me any scripture that required the person being healed to be a believer. So then, what was the purpose for signs, etc.? They were to announce the coming of the Messiah.

"…..**Your God will come with vengeance, even God with a recompense: He will come and save you. Then the eyes of the blind shall be opened, and the ears of the deft shall be unstopped. Then shall the lame man leap as an hart, and the tongue of the dumb sing: for in the wilderness shall waters break out, and streams in the desert.**" Isaiah 35:4-6

Miracles were performed by the Lord to authenticate He was Messiah. That is why John sent two of his disciples to question Jesus. "**Now when John had heard in the prison the works of Christ, he sent two of his disciples, and said unto him, Art thou He that should come, or do we look for another? Jesus answered and said unto them, Go and shew John again those things which ye do hear and see: The blind receive their sight , and the lame walk, the lepers are cleansed, and the deaf hear, the dead are raised up, and the poor have the gospel preached to them. And blessed is he, whosoever shall not be offended in me.**" Matthew 11:2-6

Pentecost was one of the seven Jewish feast days. It was held fifty days after the feast of Passover. When the feast of Pentecost was come (Acts 1) Peter and the 120 others were assembled together in what has been called the upper room. First they appointed two to be considered for taking the place left vacated by Judas. The majority vote was given to Matthias.

Then in Acts 2: 1, 3-4, "**And when the day of Pentecost was fully come, ..and there appeared unto them cloves of tongues like as of fire, and it sat upon each of them.**

And they were all filled with the Holy Ghost, and began to speak with other tongues, as the Spirit gave them utterance."

The next verses go on to say there were devout Jews from every nation under the sun there hearing everyone speaking to them in their own language. They were so astonished that this was happening, they accused them of being drunk. But Peter was not confused at all and began quoting from the Book of Joel.

"But this is that which was spoken by the prophet Joel; and it shall come to pass in the last days, saith God, I will pour out of my Spirit upon all flesh: and your sons and your daughters shall prophesy, and your young men shall see visions, and your old men shall dream dreams: and on my servants and on my handmaids I will pour out in those days of my Spirit and they shall prophesy." Acts 2: 16-18

You will note that the Spirit's coming was accompanied by a noise that sounded much like a tornado or hurricane. Anyone who has ever been around one of those two things know it is quite a wake up call; an attention getter. After getting the Jews attention, God sends a sign: a cloven tongue, like as fire, sat upon each of them. If the noise of the wind didn't get their attention, this surely would. God was sending a message to Israel: Mcssiah has come and the time for the restoration of Israel is near.

God Had promised the nation of Israel he would restore to them all lands that conquerors of the past had taken from the. (Joel 2: 25-32) This would be accomplished when He returned to establish His 1000 year reign on earth. Know what? God never promised the Gentiles that!

True, the Holy Spirit was given to some of the first Gentile converts, but not by the laying on of hands. They spoke in tongues, but this was a sign to convince the Jews that Paul's message that there was no difference between Jew and Gentile was true. You will find that after Israel was declared "Not my people," there is never a mention of tongues nor signs or miracles.

There was a very small gathering of Jews assembled in the upper room on the day of Pentecost. They were the first to see the advent of the Holy Ghost into the world. But you will only find the doctrine of the indwelling Spirit in the Pauline Epistles. In them alone will you find how you can be filled with the Spirit, quench the Spirit, be baptized by the Spirit; how we can know that the Spirit who is in us is greater than he that is in the world.

The Pauline Epistles reveal things exclusively for the age of grace; the mystery hid in God before the foundation of the world, the mystery kept secret since the world began; the formation of a new group of believers-the Church the Body of Christ.

In this dispensation of the grace of God, we do not have to ask for the outpouring of the Spirit. If we are saved, we have the indwelling Spirit with us at all times. To be filled with the Spirit, one only has to empty oneself of the flesh not speaking in tongues.

Signs were for the purpose of showing the Jews that the Messiah had come. When that had been accomplished, the sign gifts ceased. In the latest Epistles of Paul there is no mention of the sign gifts at all.

In Philippians 2: 25-29, Epaphroditus is "sick nigh unto death." Not because of any sin, but because he had been working so hard and had found that his friends were "full of heaviness" because they had heard he was sick. Why didn't Paul heal him?

In 1 Timothy 5: 23, Paul tells his beloved Timothy to quit drinking water "but use a little wine for they stomach's sake and thine often infirmities." Why didn't Paul heal him?

In 2 Timothy 4: 20, Paul had to leave Trophimus at Miletum because he was sick. Why didn't Paul heal him and take him with him on his journey? Answer! Healing was no longer included in the dispensation at hand. Paul gave Timothy a lot of instructions about what he was to do when he died, but he never left one word to him about healing.

Paul said he gloried in his infirmities. I am sure he had taught Timothy and Trophimus to do likewise. Both knowing that the sign gifts were no longer operative for them. There is no foundation in the Word of God for the prevailing Pentecostal doctrine of "divine healing."

Does God heal today? Yes He does! But His miracles are sovereign. Just because God heals someone every now and then does not mean that He will heal everyone who asks it of Him. I would not dare to limit the power of God and His ability to do whatever He wants to do. But I must warn you that teachers who say they have the power to heal are to be watched very carefully. There has been so much damage done by some of them. Remember, Satan has his ministers just as Christ has His ministers.

The following quotes are from a pamphlet by A. E. Bishop. It is published by Moody Press. I got these quotes from a pamphlet written by the late J. C, O'Hair.

1. There is a corrective passage in God's Word for every error, every heresy, every delusion, every hobby, every fanaticism and every unbalanced position.
2. For some years after Pentecost the church was exclusively Jewish, clinging to their rites and ceremonies, the converts sometimes receiving the Holy Spirit subsequent to their conversion, by the imposition of the apostolic hands. (Acts 8: 14-17)
3. There is no foundation in the Word of God for the prevailing popular doctrine of divine healing. It is not true that healing is as much the will of God for every Christian as salvation is for the unsaved. Some of the choicest of saints by the elective will of God have been patient sufferers for years upon sick beds.
4. Also after careful restudies of the book of Acts and of the Epistles written before its close, I am convinced that those who contend for a purely kingdom dispensation covering the book of Acts period are those who contend that the sign gifts are still in the church and would be in manifestation everywhere if God's people were in a healthy spiritual state and exercising faith to that end.
5. In the latest Epistles of Paul not only is it noticeable that the sign gifts are nowhere in manifestation, but a different order is brought forth by the Holy Spirit for the correction of prevailing hobbies and fanaticism.
6. A careful study of the Epistles especially of the latest Epistles of Paul, which give the normal course of the church during the present dispensation, would dismount all from their hobbies, eliminate the last vestige of Judaism from their lives and teach-

ings, and would adjust things in general, placing secondary things in their place and first things where they belong.
7. Is it the Spirit of God or Satan who attempts to revive the sign gifts that were divinely retired after having fulfilled their purpose? Every widespread attempt to revive them, has without exception, resulted in confusion, divisions, injury and disgrace.
8. This was an overlapping of the former and present dispensations, as some years elapsed before the dispensation of grace took its normal course.
9. In contrast with the sign gifts of 1 Corinthians 12, limited to a portion of the believers and operative only during the book of Acts period, let us note the non-sign gifts of Ephesians 4: 10.
10. The fact that the Bible does not give a hint of the manifestation of the sign gifts after the close of the book of Acts, must carry convincing evidence to the careful student who compares Scripture with Scripture, that they have been retired.
11. If we give heed to this fact, it will be easy for us to see later on why God, who is sovereign in the giving of signs, afterwards retired completely the sign gifts.
12. Is it the Spirit of God or Satan who turns the eyes of sincere Christians back to Pentecost and away from the goal placed before them in Ephesians, Philippians and Colossians?

Who Are We To Believe?

I want to be perfectly clear. If you want to know whether the sign gifts are for you today, study the Scriptures. Not just the ones your pastor/teacher gives you, Get a good concordance and tract down every available verse you can find on the subject. If there seems to be a contradiction between what the pastor/teacher said and the Word of God, let me give you some suggestions as to hoe you should study. First of all, ask questions:

1. Do the verses fall under the dispensation of the law or the dispensation of grace? (We are living in the dispensation of Grace.)
2. To who are the verses speaking – Jew or Gentile? While all Scripture is FOR us, remember all Scripture is not TO us in the present dispensation.
3. Do the verses you are reading seem to contradict with other verses elsewhere? If they do, you need to take the verse that is for the present dispensation. Chances are you will find that God has seen fit to do away with certain practices in the present dispensation.

Thos of us who are privileged to live in the dispensation of Grace have certain responsibilities: **Let a man so account of us, as of the ministers of Christ, and stewards of the mysteries of God. Moreover it is required in stewards, that a man be found faithful. But with me it is a very small thing that I should be judged of you, or of man's judgment: yea, I judge not mine own self. For I know nothing by myself; yet am I not hereby justified: but he that judgeth me is the Lord.** (1 Corinthians 4: 1-4)

We are to be stewards of the mysteries of God. It does not say stewards of the law. You will only find the mystery concerning the Church the Body of Christ in the Pauline Epistles. There will come a time when we will all stand before God to give an account of our stewardship, if you are found lacking of knowledge of what was expected of you, you will not escape the judgment of God by saying, "My preacher taught me differently."

God holds each and every one of us responsible for our own actions. It is time we took the responsibility for learning what is truth and what is not. Search the Scriptures. We all have a ministry. Are you performing yours? **And say to Archippus, Take heed to the ministry which thou hast received in the Lord, that thou fulfil it.** (Colossians 4: 17)

You have been given: **But unto every one of us is given grace according to the measure of the gift of Christ.** (Ephesians 4: 7) Do not overlook what you have nor neglect the responsibility that goes with it. **Study to shew thyself approved unto God, a workman that needeth not to be ashamed, rightly dividing the word of truth.** (2 Timothy 2: 15)

Chapter Six

The Gospel of the Circumcision

According to Galatians 2: 7, this gospel was committed to Peter. **But contrariwise, when they saw that the gospel of the uncircumcision was committed unto me, as the gospel of the circumcision was unto Peter;**

What is the Gospel of the Circumcision? Is it the good news we are to follow today? Is it different from the gospel of the uncircumcision given to Paul? These are questions you should be asking, and we will attempt to clear that up in this chapter.

The four gospels of Matthew, Mark, Luke and John record the commission of out Lord to go to the world and teach this gospel. You will find them in Matthew 28: 19-20, Mark 16: 14-18, Luke 22: 44-47 and John 20: 19-23. Since the account in Matthew is better known, let us examine it. Many call this the Great Commission: **Go ye therefore, and teach all nations, baptizing them in the name of the Father, and of the Son, and of the Holy Ghost: Teaching them** to observe all things whatsoever I have commanded you: and, lo, I am with you alway, even unto the end of the world. Amen. (Matthew 28: 19-20)

These are the marching orders for the gospel of the circumcision. Look at what they say.

1. Go and teach all nations and baptize them. Teach them what?
2. Teach them to observe all the things that Christ taught and commanded of them.

The baptismal message they were to teach was nothing new. It was the same message that John the Baptist began preaching prior to the ministry of Jesus: **And he came into all the country about Jordan, preaching the baptism of repentance for the remission of sins;** (Luke 3: 3) It is also the message that Peter preached in Acts 2: 38: **Then Peter said unto them, Repent, and be baptized every one of you in the name of Jesus Christ for the remission of sins, and ye shall receive the gift of the Holy Ghost.**

John the Baptist and Peter were definitely teaching the same kind of baptism, were they not? What about marching order number two? Do you really know what Jesus taught His disciples? Probably not, so let's do a quick run though of all He taught in the book of Matthew.

Matthew 2: 2: **Saying, Where is he that is born King of the Jews? for we have seen his star in the east, and are come to worship him.** Even though this is not a command of Jesus, it does give us some insight into the overall theme of the book. Israel had been looking for a king to come and restore them to their rightful earthly inheritance.

Matthew 3: 2-3: **And saying, Repent ye: for the kingdom of heaven is at hand. For this is he that was spoken of by the prophet Esaias, saying, The voice of one crying in the wilderness, Prepare ye the way of the Lord, make his paths straight.** John the Baptist is declaring that the long awaited kingdom was close at hand and that the Messiah spoken of by Isaiah had arrived.

Matthew 3: 13-15: **Then cometh Jesus from Galilee to Jordan unto John, to be baptized of him. But John forbad him, saying, I have need to be baptized of thee, and comest thou to me? And Jesus answering said unto him, Suffer it to be so now: for thus it becometh us to fulfil all righteousness. Then he suffered him.** Jesus had no sins, so why was He asking to be baptized? Answer: To fulfill all righteousness. The law required baptism. Jesus placed Himself under the laws of man and had to do all the law required.

Matthew 4: 17: **From that time Jesus began to preach, and to say, Repent: for the kingdom of heaven is at hand.** The kingdom of heaven spoken of in the passage is the 1,000 year millennial kingdom, an earthly kingdom.

Matthew 4: 23: **And Jesus went about all Galilee, teaching in their synagogues, and preaching the gospel of the kingdom, and healing all manner of sickness and all manner of disease among the people.** This is the same gospel but now He is beginning to perform the miracles that prophets of old had foretold would be a sign to Israel of Messiah's eminent return.

Matthew 5: 2, 5: **And he opened his mouth, and taught them, saying ...Blessed are the meek: for they shall inherit**

the earth. What is the teaching concerning the kingdom of heaven? It is on earth.

Matthew 5: 17-18: **Think not that I am come to destroy the law, or the prophets: I am not come to destroy, but to fulfil. For verily I say unto you, Till heaven and earth pass, one jot or one tittle shall in no wise pass from the law, till all be fulfilled.** The declaration of Jesus is that He came to fulfill the law. It is obvious that the law was still operative.

Matthew 6: 10: **Thy kingdom come, Thy will be done in earth, as it is in heaven**. When teaching His disciple what has come to be known as the Lord's prayer, He instructed to pray for the kingdom on earth to come.

Matthew 6: 14-15: **For if ye forgive men their trespasses, your heavenly Father will also forgive you: But if ye forgive not men their trespasses, neither will your Father forgive your trespasses.** Check it out! Forgiveness of sins could not take place as long as you had not forgiven others for any sins against you. Is that true today? It is not.

Matthew 10: 5-6: **These twelve Jesus sent forth, and commanded them, saying, <u>Go not into</u> the way of the <u>Gentiles</u>, and into any city of the Samaritans enter ye not: But go rather to the lost sheep of the house of Israel.** Does Jesus say stay away from the Gentiles? Isn't that strange? No, it is not. Israel must be converted so she can become a blessing to the world, and the world come to the knowledge of God through Israel.

Matthew 10: 9-10: **Provide neither gold, nor silver, nor brass in your purses, Nor scrip for your journey, neither two coats, neither shoes, nor yet staves: for the workman**

is worthy of his meat. Do you know many preachers today that have little thought for money? They are one in a million. Then why were they instructed to teach this? In the new kingdom, of which they were to be a part, there would be no need for anything because everything would be provided for them.

Matthew 12: 39: **But he answered and said unto them, An evil and adulterous generation seeketh after a sign; and there shall no sign be given to it, but the sign of the prophet Jonas:** So why do men look for signs today? They must be evil and adulterous or have listen to evil teaches and believed what they said. How many denominations do you know of who are advocates of the sign gifts?

Matthew 15: 22-26: **And, behold, a woman of Canaan came out of the same coasts, and cried unto him, saying, Have mercy on me, O Lord, thou Son of David; my daughter is grievously vexed with a devil. But he answered her not a word. And his disciples came and besought him, saying, Send her away; for she crieth after us. But he answered and said, <u>I am not sent but unto the lost sheep of the house of Israel</u>. Then came she and worshipped him, saying, Lord, help me. But he answered and said, <u>It is not meet to take the children's bread, and to cast it to dogs</u>.** There are several things in these verses you need to look at carefully. The lady asked for mercy and called Him Lord. He did not even answer her at first but when He did He told her he was not sent to Gentiles – He was sent to Israel. Bread refers to salvation, which He said should not be given to Gentile dogs before Israel had received it. Is that the message for today? It is not. But at the time Jesus spoke the words it was the program of the day and His disciples were instructed to follow that program.

Matthew 16: 21-23: **From that time forth began Jesus to shew unto his disciples, how that he must go unto Jerusalem, and suffer many things of the elders and chief priests and scribes, and be killed, and be raised again the third day. Then Peter took him, and began to rebuke him, saying, Be it far from thee, Lord: this shall not be unto thee. But he turned, and said unto Peter, Get thee behind me, Satan: thou art an offence unto me: for thou savourest not the things that be of God, but those that be of men.** Can you believe it? The disciples had no idea what Jesus was talking about. They did not understand anything about the death, burial and resurrection that was to come. Why? Luke 18: 31-34 says it was hid from them. In other words it was a mystery hid in Scripture and they were not to understand it at the time.

Matthew 24: 13: **But he that shall endure unto the end, the same shall be saved.** Those who do not believe in eternal security use this to state their case. It is sad they do not realize this message was to Israel and has no such application under the message of grace in the present dispensation.

Matthew 24: 14: **And this gospel of the kingdom shall be preached in all the world for a witness unto all nations; and then shall the end come.** Matthew 24: 13-14 was a part of the gospel of the circumcision. The Jew will live with Christ for 1,000 years on the earth. That is their inheritance but it is not ours.

The sixteen items listed above paint a clear picture of what Jesus taught and did during His three year ministry on earth. He chose twelve men to carry out the work He had begun. He trained them, taught them everything they needed to know to carry out the task that was before them. What He did not want them to know He kept hid from them. What they were instructed to do is clear:

1. They were to teach – "Repent and be baptized for the remission of sins." (Matt. 28: 19-20; Acts 2: 38)
2. They were to begin their ministry at Jerusalem. (Luke 24: 47)
3. They were to wait for the power that would come from the Holy Spirit before they were to begin their ministry. (Acts 1: 8) They had already received the Spirit (John 20: 22) but now they were to wait for the power to come.
4. Once they had that power, they were given instructions as to where they should begin their ministry: beginning at Jerusalem, then to all Judea, then to Samaria, and after all that to go to the uttermost parts of the earth. (acts 1: 8)
   (Let me explain Acts 1: 8. Judea and Samaria were the Southern and Northern sections of Israel. The disciples were instructed to begin their ministry in Jerusalem and then go to the rest of the Jewish nation before seeking out Jews in the rest of the world.)
5. They were to teach everything the Lord had commanded them to do. (Matt. 28: 19-20)
6. As a part of that command, they were to tell everyone who would listen that the kingdom of heaven, which was on earth, was at hand. If one wanted to be a part of that kingdom, one would have to repent and be baptized and believe what the prophets of old foretold. Peter said as much in Acts 2: 16-30.
7. When the people of that day asked what one needed to do to be saved (Acts 2: 37), Peter said repent and be baptized. (Acts 2: 38) One does not need to be baptized today in order to obtain a heavenly inheritance with God.

The Gospel of the Uncircumcision

But contrariwise, when they saw that the gospel of the uncircumcision was committed unto me, as the gospel of the circumcision was unto Peter; (Galatians 2: 7) The gospel of the uncircumcision was committed unto Paul. Contrary to Peter's gospel, which was to the circumcision (Jews), Paul's gospel was to the Gentiles: **For I speak to you Gentiles, inasmuch as I am the apostle of the Gentiles, I magnify mine office:** (Romans 11: 13)

Whereas Peter's gospel message was to "repent and be baptized," Paul's gospel was just the opposite: **For Christ sent me not to baptize, but to preach the gospel: not with wisdom of words, lest the cross of Christ should be made of none effect.** (1 Corinthians 1: 17)

Peter's gospel was centered on prophetic things concerning Israel's restoration; Paul's gospel was center on things kept secret, both those hid in Scripture and those hid in God.

The Mystery Hid in Scripture

Now to him that is of power to stablish you according to my gospel, and the preaching of Jesus Christ, according to the revelation of the mystery, which was kept secret since the world began, But now is made manifest, and by the scriptures of the prophets, according to the commandment of the everlasting God, made known to all nations for the obedience of faith: (Romans 16: 25-26)

What was Paul's Gospel? It is define in 1 Corinthians 15: 1-4: **Moreover, brethren, I declare unto you the gospel which I preached unto you, which also ye have received, and wherein ye stand; By which also ye are saved, if ye**

keep in memory what I preached unto you, unless ye have believed in vain. For I delivered unto you first of all that which I also received, how that Christ died for our sins according to the scriptures; And that he was buried, and that he rose again the third day according to the scriptures:

This Gospel was hidden in Old Testament Scripture, as in Isaiah 53. While Old Testament Scripture tells of the death of Christ and John the Baptist said "**Behold the Lamb of God, which taketh away the sins of the world,**" (John 1: 29) neither Isaiah nor John say that is good news. Why? God had chosen to keep the meaning of certain Scripture a secret, as is stated in 1 Corinthians 2: 7-8: **But we speak the wisdom of God in a mystery, even the hidden [wisdom], which God ordained before the world unto our glory: Which none of the princes of this world knew: for had they known it, they would not have crucified the Lord of glory.**

Before God created the world, He planned to have Jesus come to earth and die for man's sins. Even though He planned it before He created Adam and recorded it in Old Testament Scripture, He chose to keep its meaning a secret until He raised up Paul as the apostle to the Gentiles. Had God not done so, Satan would not have plotted to have Him killed, knowing it would be his demise.

God's wisdom surpasses all other wisdom. Even though Lucifer was the wisest of all of God's creation, his wisdom pales when compared with the wisdom of God. 1 Corinthians 1: 18-24: **For the preaching of the cross is to them that perish foolishness; but unto us which are saved it is the power of God. For it is written, I will destroy the wisdom of the wise, and will bring to nothing the understanding of the prudent. Where is the wise? where is the scribe?**

where is the disputer of this world? hath not God made foolish the wisdom of this world? For after that in the wisdom of God the world by wisdom knew not God, it pleased God by the foolishness of preaching to save them that believe. For the Jews require a sign, and the Greeks seek after wisdom: But we preach Christ crucified, unto the Jews a stumblingblock, and unto the Greeks foolishness; But unto them which are called, both Jews and Greeks, Christ the power of God, and the wisdom of God.

Paul's Gospel of the Uncircumcision is about:

1. Christ dying for our sins.
2. Christ being buried, and
3. Christ being resurrected from the grave on the third day.

In Ephesians 6: 19-20 Paul asks people to pray for him to have boldness to preach about the mystery (secret) of the gospel. Look at the verses: **And for me, that utterance may be given unto me, that I may open my mouth boldly, to make known the mystery of the gospel, For which I am an ambassador in bonds: that therein I may speak boldly, as I ought to speak.**

So Paul was talking about the secret of the good news (Gospel). That secret had been hidden and now it became Paul's responsibility to tell others about the good news. Why would he need boldness to teach Christ died for your sins? Because the Jews believed that salvation for the world would come through the nation of Israel, and it did at one point in time. The good news is that Christ is all you need was kept a secret. You will not find that anywhere but in the Pauline epistles.

Oh, there is plenty of good news in all of the Bible, but none like the good news revealed unto Paul. The good news God revealed to Paul is centered on Christ, not Israel. No longer was the blessing of God predicated on one blessing Israel, as you see in Genesis 12: 3: **And I will bless them that bless thee, and curse him that curseth thee: and in thee shall all families of the earth be blessed.**

True, Christ is the seed of Abraham and all who trust Christ as Savior will be blessed. But salvation, in the Age of Grace, is accomplished through the death of Christ and not through Israel. You do not have to love or bless Israel to receive the gift of salvation, all you need to do is accept what Christ did for you. That was the mystery of the good news. The revelation that the cross was the focal point in God's plan for salvation was a shock to the Jewish religious order. Jesus was a threat to that order and that is why they plotted to kill Him.

Peter delivers a stirring message to Israel in Acts 2 and 3. He told them the nation denied the Holy One and set a murderer free. He told them they killed the Prince of Life but God had raised Him from the dead. He also said, "I know you did it through ignorance." But what He doesn't say is very important to understanding why his gospel is not for us today. Peter does not say that salvation is believing Christ died for your sins when the people asked what they must do, he says: **Then Peter said unto them, Repent, and be baptized every one of you in the name of Jesus Christ for the remission of sins, and ye shall receive the gift of the Holy Ghost.** (Acts 2: 38)

Then he says: **Repent ye therefore, and be converted, that your sins may be blotted out, when the times of refreshing shall come from the presence of the Lord; And he shall** send Jesus Christ, which before was preached unto you: Whom the heaven must receive until the times of restitution of all things, which God hath spoken by the mouth of all his holy prophets since the world began.** (Acts 3: 19-21)

Peter doesn't say your sins will be blotted out the moment you trust Christ as Savior; he says your sins will not be blotted out until Christ returns to earth the second time. That will be just prior to the 1,000 year millennial reign. Peter's statement is absolutely true, for that particular group of people, but it is not true for us today. Israel's sins will not be blotted out until Christ returns to earth again.

Those who are saved believing the gospel Paul preached are:

> **"Justified by His blood"** Romans 5: 9.
> **"Reconciled to God by the death of His Son"** Romans 5: 10.
> **"Have redemption through His blood"** Ephesians 1: 7, and
> **"Are made neigh by the blood of Christ"** Ephesians 2: 13.

The mystery of the good news Paul preached is centered in Christ and on His death, burial and resurrection. The Scriptures tell about the death of Christ, but until God revealed that to Paul it was nor known.

It was not know by Peter in Acts 1-8 because Paul is not saved until Acts 9. Paul was the one who made known the mystery; he was God's ambassador to make it known: **And for me, that utterance may be given unto me, that I may open my mouth boldly, to make known the mystery of** the gospel, For which I am an ambassador in bonds: that therein I may speak boldly, as I ought to speak. (Ephesians 6: 19-20)

The story of Paul's conversion is found in Acts 9: 3-5; 13-16: **And as he journeyed, he came near Damascus: and suddenly there shined round about him a light from heaven: And he fell to the earth, and heard a voice saying unto him, Saul, Saul, why persecutest thou me? And he said, Who art thou, Lord? And the Lord said, I am Jesus whom thou persecutest: it is hard for thee to kick against the pricks. ... Then Ananias answered, Lord, I have heard by many of this man, how much evil he hath done to thy saints at Jerusalem: And here he hath authority from the chief priests to bind all that call on thy name. But the Lord said unto him, Go thy way: for he is a chosen vessel unto me, to bear my name before the Gentiles, and kings, and the children of Israel: For I will shew him how great things he must suffer for my name's sake.**

He tells King Agrippa about his conversion in Acts 26: 13-18: **At midday, O king, I saw in the way a light from heaven, above the brightness of the sun, shining round about me and them which journeyed with me. And when we were all fallen to the earth, I heard a voice speaking unto me, and saying in the Hebrew tongue, Saul, Saul, why persecutest thou me? it is hard for thee to kick against the pricks. And I said, Who art thou, Lord? And he said, I am Jesus whom thou persecutest. But rise, and stand upon thy feet: for I have appeared unto thee for this purpose, to make thee a minister and a witness both of these things which thou hast seen, and of those things in the which I will appear unto thee; Delivering thee from the people, and from the Gentiles, unto whom now I send thee, To open their eyes, and to**

turn them from darkness to light, and from the power of Satan unto God, that they may receive forgiveness of sins, and inheritance among them which are sanctified by faith that is in me.

Paul began his ministry to the Gentiles as the Lord instructed him, but everywhere he taught the Jews caused problems for him. On one occasion the Lord, in a vision, warned him to leave Jerusalem: **And it came to pass, that, when I was come again to Jerusalem, even while I prayed in the temple, I was in a trance; And saw him saying unto me, Make haste, and get thee quickly out of Jerusalem: for they will not receive thy testimony concerning me. And I said, Lord, they know that I imprisoned and beat in every synagogue them that believed on thee: And when the blood of thy martyr Stephen was shed, I also was standing by, and consenting unto his death, and kept the raiment of them that slew him. And he said unto me, Depart: for I will send thee far hence unto the Gentiles.**

During the time of his ministry Paul was always defending the message of grace. In his letter to the Galatians he is concerned:

1. That those at Galatia had departed from what he taught them about Christ and were being led to believe another gospel. (Galatians 1: 6-9)
2. He tells the Galatians the gospel he preached came from God and not men. (Gal. 1: 11-12)
3. He tells them he had gone to Jerusalem and communicated t5he gospel he preached among the Gentiles. However, he said he had to speak privately to the Jews or his efforts would have been in vain. (Gal. 2: 1-2)

4. Then he says that Peter, James and John accepted the fact that he was to preach to the Gentiles and they preach to the Jews. (Gal. 2: 7-9)
5. He explains it is Christ's faith that saves, not man's faith. (Gal. 2: 16)
6. Paul declares that no man is justified by the law. (Gal. 3: 11)
7. He also said the law was a curse and that Christ had redeemed mankind from that curse. (Gal. 3: 13)
8. He also states that men had been kept under the law and shut up to the faith of Christ that was to be revealed. (Gal. 3: 23)
9. He states that the law was only a schoolmaster to point us to Christ, and after Christ exercised His faith to die, we did not need he law anymore. (Gal. 3: 24-25)
10. Then Paul encouraged them to stand fast in the liberty of the grace of God and challenged them to not go back to the bondage of the law; for if you do your will prostitute the grace of God. (Gal. 5: 1-4)
11. He closed the letter to the Galatians by saying it is not circumcision or uncircumcision that matters at all, but become a new creature in Christ. (Gal. 6: 15)

The gospel of the uncircumcision is about becoming a new creature. **Therefore if any man be in Christ, he is a new creature: old things are passed away; behold, all things are become new.** (2 Corinthians 5: 17) The word creature comes from the Greek word *ktisis*: which is translated as an original formation.

In algebra, $X + X = 2X$; $2X + 2Y = 2XY$. Thinking in algebraic terms, the formula for a new creature would be $X +$

Y = Z. The Church the Body of Christ is a brand spanking new formation, a new formula. You do not take a Jew and a Gentile and get Jews and Gentiles united together. You take Jews and Gentiles and get a group of believers that are one in Christ but are neither Jew nor Gentile.

The Mystery Hid in God

What is it? Look at Ephesians 3: 1-9: **For this cause I Paul, the prisoner of Jesus Christ for you Gentiles, If ye have heard of the dispensation of the grace of God which is given me to you-ward: How that by revelation he made known unto me the mystery; (as I wrote afore in few words, Whereby, when ye read, ye may understand my knowledge in the mystery of Christ) Which in other ages was not made known unto the sons of men, as it is now revealed unto his holy apostles and prophets by the Spirit; That the Gentiles should be fellowheirs, and of the same body, and partakers of his promise in Christ by the gospel: Whereof I was made a minister, according to the gift of the grace of God given unto me by the effectual working of his power. Unto me, who am less than the least of all saints, is this grace given, that I should preach among the Gentiles the unsearchable riches of Christ; And to make all men see what is the fellowship of the mystery, which from the beginning of the world hath been <u>hid in God</u>, who created all things by Jesus Christ:**

God hid the fact that Gentiles would be saved apart form going through Israel. But after Acts 28, Israel is declare Loammi and now the hidden comes to the forefront. God reveals to Paul what he had "hid in Him" since before the foundation of the world. **Wherefore remember, that ye being in time past Gentiles in the flesh, who are called**

Uncircumcision by that which is called the Circumcision in the flesh made by hands; That at that time ye were without Christ, being aliens from the commonwealth of Israel, and strangers from the covenants of promise, having no hope, and without God in the world: But now in Christ Jesus ye who sometimes were far off are made nigh by the blood of Christ. (Eph. 2: 11-13)

Comparing the Gospel of the Circumcision with the Gospel of the Uncircumcision

Gospel of the Circumcision	Gospel of the Uncircumcision
1. Inheritance I earthly Jeremiah 23: 5-6 Matthew 5: 5; 6: 10	Inheritance – heavenly Ephesians 1: 3; 2: 6 Colossians 3: 1-3
2. Christ is King Matthew 2: 2	Christ – head of the Body Eph. 1: 22-23; Col. 1: 18
3. Prophesied in Scripture Since the world began Acts 3: 21	Hid in God before the foundation of the world Ephesians 3: 9 Chosen before the Foundation of the world Ephesians 1: 4
4. Concerns Israel (A nation) Ezekiel 37: 21-23	Concerns Jew & Gentile (A body) 1 Cor. 12: 13; Rom. 10: 12
5. Gentile blessing came Through Israel Isaiah 60: 1-3	Gentile blessing came through fall of Israel Romans 11: 11-12
6. The message, Repent & Be baptized (Acts 2: 38)	The message – not to baptize 1 Corinthians 1: 17

7. Committed to the 12	Committed to Paul
Matt. 10: 5-8, 16-20	Gal. 2: 7; Eph. 3: 1-2, 8-9;
Galatians 2: 7	Colossians 1: 25-26

In the Dispensation of Grace the Gospel of the Uncircumcision teaches:

1. Jew and Gentile are made one by Spirit baptism. 1 Corinthians 12: 13, 27.
2. Christ is the head of the body. Ephesians 1: 22-23.
3. Our inheritance is heavenly. Ephesians 1: 3.
4. We are to set our affection on heavenly, not earthly things. Colossians 3: 1-3. We are told to forget the things Christ did on earth. 2 Corinthians 2: 16. We are to remember what transpired after His death and not the things He did in the flesh.
5. We are complete in Christ. Colossians 2: 9-14.

When Christ rose from the grave He defeated Satan and He delivered us from the bondage of the law (Eph. 2: 15). We are complete in Him, risen with Him and seated in heavenly places with Him.

Man and his religious organizations want you to "do things, suggesting that mere faith alone can never satisfy God. Then they quote James 2, which says faith without works is dead. What they fail to realize, or perhaps refuse to accept, is Colossians 2: 9-14 and Ephesians 2: 15 say something different. And those books were written specifically to we Gentiles, James was written to those under the law.

I am complete in Christ. The dictionary defines complete as: having all necessary or normal parts, components, or steps:

entire; whole; having come to an end; concluded; thorough; consummate: complete control.

I am crucified with Christ: nevertheless I live; yet not I, but Christ liveth in me: and the life which I now live in the flesh I live by the faith of the Son of God, who loved me, and gave himself for me. (Galatians 2: 20)

Paul speaks of the last days for the body of Christ in 2 Timothy 3: 1-5: **This know also, that in the last days perilous times shall come. For men shall be lovers of their own selves, covetous, boasters, proud, blasphemers, disobedient to parents, unthankful, unholy, Without natural affection, trucebreakers, false accusers, incontinent, fierce, despisers of those that are good, Traitors, heady, highminded, lovers of pleasures more than lovers of God; Having a form of godliness, but denying the power thereof: from such turn away.**

Most fundamental churches teach a revival will occur before Christ returns. That will be the case before His 2nd coming, but the church will be raptured before that time and we will see churches in a state of apostasy. Look at how he describes it in 2 Timothy 4: 3-4: **For the time will come when they will not endure sound doctrine; but after their own lusts shall they heap to themselves teachers, having itching ears; And they shall turn away their ears from the truth, and shall be turned unto fables**.

The elected leadership of this country has allowed Satan a foothold in government. They have eliminated prayer in public schools, they have taken out "one nation under God" from the pledge of allegiance, they are debating the removal of "In God we Trust" from our currency, they have made states remove any copy of the ten commandment from public buildings, they have prohibited the displaying of the Nativity scene in public places and soon they will not permit the name God to be aired on radio and TV.

If that is not apostasy, what is it? I believe we are nearing the time when God will be as fed up with us as He was with Israel and will called His own to meet Him in the air. Who is responsible for the debacle? We are. We do not question the teaching emanating from the pulpits across the land. We accept what they say without checking the Scripture to see that what they are saying is what God's word says. Let these preachers be accursed. You must never forget that Satan has his ministers and I would venture to say the number of them in church pulpits will boggle your mind.

The world is being led astray by apostate preachers who try to mix the things of the law with grace. We cannot do anything in the flesh which will satisfy God. That includes water baptism, speaking in tongues, walking down an isle or praying through until you receive the victory. God has already given us the victory, his name is Jesus Christ. The works of man are filth in the eyes of God. If man thinks by doing works he can please God or that his works will save him, man has been hoodwinked. Put your trust in no man. Put your trust in God.

The Right Approach to Studying the Bible

The Bible is a wonderful book full of inspiring words. For those of us who believe it is the Word of God, it not only inspires us but fills us with joy and hope. However, there are far too many who question the validity of the Word of God, saying they are but words that men wrote. The Bible is God speaking to us.

The Bible says what it says and is not open to speculation or private interpretation. True, a verse may speak to you in some significant way which may differ from the way it affects someone else, but that does not alter what the words are. As one grows in the knowledge of the Lord a particular passage of Scripture may suddenly turn a light on to a deeper understanding of God's purpose for your life.

For example: I love to listen to different types of music: country, gospel, classical oldies of the 5o's. I can even read music. However, when it comes to the science and theory of music I am completely ignorant.

I may listen to and enjoy a great classical melody because it is beautiful and soothing to the ear; another person may hear the same song and it does nothing for them. It is boring, too melodic, without beat or rhythm. A third person, a trained musician, will hear the same piece and every note and phrase are meaningful.

The music was the same regardless of how the three of us perceived it. Our individual interpretation of the song did not mean the writer did not know or understand music, he did. He wrote it. What it does mean is two of the hearers were not qualified to make a fair appraisal of what the writer intended. The music was there for all three to hear, but only one was tuned into its full meaning.

That is how it is with the Bible. The words are simple, with a clear fixed meaning, but they are oftentimes twisted to fit theories or one's own convictions. Does that make the Bible wrong, or the interpretation wrong? Fact: God is never wrong.

There is the real and the unreal in today's world. Men will continue to "buy" both as long as there are those offering them a choice. You can buy imitation pearls for just a few dollars and you can find them almost anywhere. Real pearls are more expensive and their supply is often times limited. The same is true about the Bible. Many will "buy into" the imitation because of their abundance, but the real Bible is not stocked in great supply. The King James Bible is the word of God, not the New King James, the Old King James.

The false teachers of this world win converts to their cause by discrediting the real Bible, saying the Bible is unreliable in that it contradicts itself. They go even further with words like, "Anyone with any intelligence would dismiss mush of the Scripture as a myth or old wives tales." Yet Jesus said the word of God is written top be understood by babes, not the wise: **At that time Jesus answered and said, I thank thee, O Father, Lord of heaven and earth, because thou hast hid these things from the wise and prudent, and hast revealed them unto babes.** (Matthew 11: 25)

So what are we trying to get across to you? The Bible contains many wonderful things which only a child of God is equipped to understand. Babes accept the truth because their minds are open and have not been clutter by the thoughts of men. Babes are teachable because they do not have things to unlearn. The Bible was written for hearts willing to receive, willing to learn and willing to prepare to be fit for service. Too many choose not to hear: **And when Jesus knew [it], he saith unto them, Why reason ye, because ye have no bread? perceive ye not yet, neither understand? have ye your heart yet hardened? Having eyes, see ye not? and having ears, hear ye not? and do ye not remember?** (Mark 8: 17-18)

Helen Rowland Promell penned the following:

> Grandfather has grown dull of ear
> He claims that he can scarcely
> Hear the words we speak,
> Unless we shout
> And aid our speech by pointing out
> And indicating what we say
> With gestures made a certain way.
>
> But go with him in any wood,
> And, though his hearing is not good,
> He listens to the talk of trees,
> And nods agreement to the bees,
> And says he knows
> The clear-cut note
> Each Harebell holds within its throat
> Which sounds whenever Harebells sway
> In rhythm with a breezy day.
>
> I cannot catch a thing he hears.
> It makes me wonder if his ears
> Have grown beyond the commonplace,
> And are attuned with time and space
> Outrunning ordinary kin
> Of all of us who,
> Would give a lot if we could hear
> The music of some unknown sphere.

To understand the deeper truths of the Bible one must get his heart and mind conditioned to receive them. First you have to believe in order to hear. Jesus said: **… everyone who is of truth heareth my voice.**" (John 18: 37b) The verse implies there are some who cannot hear the truth of the Word. Only those of truth (the saved) can hear.

Unbelievers can read the Bible, but cannot understand the hidden truths reserved for the believer. To the lost, the Bible seems confusing, hard to read and outdated. So, men oftentimes fabricate their own book, such as Joseph Smith, who supposedly found some ancient tablets which he transcribe into the Book of Mormons. He later got some revelation from God and wrote Doctrine and Covenants and The Pearl of Great Price. Mormons think the Bible is holy, but it assumes second place to the book by Joseph Smith.

I have some friends who are Mormons. They are some of the nicest people I have ever met. They are very family oriented and have high morals; they are very good people. But I believe if they think the words of Joseph Smith should take precedence over God's word, they are deceived. I am not saying they are not saved, they are if they have believed the gospel, but they may not have a clear understanding of truth found only in God's words.

Joseph Smith does not stand alone in this arena of false teaching or false books . The Catholic church has its missals, the Baptist, Methodist, Presbyterians, Episcopalians, Church of Christ, Christian Church, Pentecostal and most all other denominations have their very own creeds that are oftentimes revered more than the Word of God. If any denomination places their creed or words of their leaders above the Word of God, they are not to be trusted.

The real Bible is for those who have eyes to see, ears to hear and hearts that welcome truth, from it comes forth a light so bright that shines like a beacon that guides ships through a foggy night. When the Bible speaks to you it will speak with a voice, not muffled, but with a sound so magnificent and loud it would astonish those who frequent rock concerts.

Clara H. Scott wrote the following song, Open My Eyes. Open my eyes, that I may see glimpses of truth thou hast for me; place in my hands the wonderful key that shall unclasp and set me free. Silently now I wait for thee, ready my God thy will to see; open my eyes, illumine me, Spirit divine.

Open my mouth and let me bear gladly the warm truth everywhere; open my heart and let me prepare love with thy children thus to share. Silently now I wait for thee, ready my God thy will to see; open my eyes, illumine me, Spirit divine.

Ms Scott knew she must be willing to open her eyes to see truth before she could share the message of truth. To be spiritually illuminated by the Word of God, there must first be an enlightening of the mind by the Holy Spirit. That only comes with study. **Study to shew thyself approved unto God, a workman that needeth not to be ashamed, rightly dividing the word of truth.** (2 Timothy 2: 15)

To the saved person, the Words of God are treasures above monetary value, but to the lost, they are just words. To the children of darkness the Bible is nothing more than a novel they may have read, but for the children of light it is a symphony played by a 1,000 stringed orchestra. The Spirit which inspired the writers of Scripture waits to illuminate the children of light.

But as it is written, Eye hath not seen, nor ear heard, neither have entered into the heart of man, the things which God hath prepared for them that love him. But God hath revealed them unto us by his Spirit: for the Spirit searcheth all things, yea, the deep things of God. For what man knoweth the things of a man, save the spirit of man which is in him? even so the things of God

knoweth no man, but the Spirit of God. Now we have received, not the spirit of the world, but the spirit which is of God; that we might know the things that are freely given to us of God. (1 Corinthians 2: 9-12)

Once you have prepared your heart to receive truth, then commit yourself to studying the Word on a regular basis. Understand that the entire Bible is FOR you, but there are some books written specifically TO you. For the saved of the 21st century, the books written by Paul, Romans through Philemon, are the books written specifically TO you.

Too many people get saved but never grow in the knowledge of truth. One of the reason they do not grow is they do not serve. Serve the Lord, and you begin that by studying. Once you have learned something, share it with someone else. The more you learn and share, the more you grow. Go out and have fun, child of God, for God wants your service for him to be enjoyable.

Restoration

Think on These Things

What kind of person would we be if we agreed to make life-changing decisions based upon hearsay? We would be foolish. Decisions that affect what a company will pursue, invest in, and lay its reputation on the line requires diligent study and long hours of debating the pros and cons.

If it is important to be prudent and resolute in business, why shouldn't it be of equal importance in things spiritual? Why are we so ambitious in things related to business and so lazy in the pursuit of understanding the Word of God?

You might think you are ambitious in your Bible study when in fact you are not a studier but a reader. You might think you have a good understanding of truth but you do not. "What makes you say that," you ask? Let me ask you a question. "This knowledge that you say you have, how did you acquire it? Did you receive it from parents, from a Sunday School teacher, a preacher, rabbi, priest, a denominational creed or a friend?"

Now any and all of these may be reliable sources of information, but then again they may not be. I would need to know where they obtained their information before I could be sure of it authenticity. I would want to know if theses sources obtained their data from hearsay or from actual study.

Wouldn't it be wise to be as prudent and resolute in the things that will affect your spiritual life, at least on an equal basis with the things that affect a business? It should be, so why not take the same approach as you would in business: study, diligently, spend long hours sorting out all the pros and cons.

Pentecost

For most Christians, this is a word that has significance. What mental picture do you get when you see it in print or hear it spoken? Do you recall when you first heard about it? I imagine that if you have heard of it you probably received your knowledge of it through some traditional form of church teaching. You have probably accepted whatever the authoritative figure at home or church told you. In other words, if it was good enough for Mom and Dad, it's good enough for me syndrome.

So, perhaps you have been told that Pentecost marks the beginning of the Church the Body of Christ; that on this day there were assembled Jews and Gentiles having all things common and thus establishing the way Christians should conduct themselves in the 21st Century. You were probably told that the events that transpired on the day of Pentecost, the outpouring of the Holy Spirit, the speaking in tongues, the healing of the sick, raising of the dead, etc. are things that we can do ourselves today. Are they?

If you want to be a workman that needeth not to be ashamed you will learn to rightly divide the truth. (2 Timothy 2: 15) You will have to come to the decision that there must be a Book that has the truth in it, and for me it is a King James Bible. You must also believe what the Word says, not what flesh and blood said. I will be the first to admit that this may be difficult because it may mean admitting you have been wrong for many years.

Do you realize how hard it is to admit you may have been wrong? It is as hard as it is for most of us to say I'm sorry. But if you really want to know the truth about Biblical things, you must ask yourselves some serious questions:

1. Do I really want to know the truth if it means I may be the object of ridicule? I can assure you there will be many that will ridicule you, perhaps curse you and call you names if you go against the way they believe.
2. Do I really want to be satisfied with the limited knowledge I have even if it is wrong?
3. Do I want to know what God has for me or will I be content in having a small portion?

Suffering for the truth is nothing new, most true believers have had to suffer. Jesus Christ chose to suffer, and you and I have been called on to suffer with the promise of reigning with Christ if we do. (2 Timothy 2: 12)

THE STARTING POINT

Before we can get a clear picture of the events that transpired on the day of Pentecost (Acts 2) we need to understand why the Jews were gather together and for what purpose. Was it a law, or was it just a church fellowship? Please read Leviticus 23: 15-21:

> 15 And ye shall count unto you from the morrow after the sabbath, from the day that ye brought the sheaf of the wave offering; seven sabbaths shall be complete:
> 16 Even unto the morrow after the seventh sabbath shall ye number fifty days; and ye shall offer a new meat offering unto the Lord.
> 17 Ye shall bring out of your habitations two wave loaves of two tenth deals: they shall be of fine flour; they shall be baken with leaven; they are the firstfruits unto the Lord.
> 18 And ye shall offer with the bread seven lambs without blemish of the first year, and one young bullock, and two rams: they shall be for a burnt offering unto the Lord, with their meat offering, and their drink offerings, even an offering made by fire, of sweet savour unto the Lord.
> 19 Then ye shall sacrifice one kid of the goats for a sin offering, and two lambs of the first year for a sacrifice of peace offerings.
> 20 And the priest shall wave them with the bread of the firstfruits for a wave offering before the Lord, with the two lambs: they
> 21 And ye shall proclaim on the selfsame day, that it may be an holy convocation unto you: ye shall do no servile work therein: it shall be a statute for ever in all your dwellings throughout your generations.

Fact: Pentecost was one of the seven Jewish feast days. It is a part of the harvest which begins with the Feast of First Fruits; "**Speak unto the children of Israel, and say unto** them, **When ye be come into the land which I give unto you, and shall reap the harvest thereof, then ye shall bring a sheaf of the firstfruits of your harvest unto the priest:"** (Leviticus 23: 10) and it ends with the Feast of Trumpets **"And when ye reap the harvest of your land, thou shalt not make clean riddance of the corners of thy field when thou reapest, neither shalt thou gather any gleaning of thy harvest: thou shalt leave them unto the poor, and to the stranger: I am the Lord your God. And the Lord spake unto Moses, saying, Speak unto the children of Israel, saying, In the seventh month, in the first day of the month, shall ye have a sabbath, a memorial of blowing of trumpets, an holy convocation. Ye shall do no servile work therein: but ye shall offer an offering made by fire unto the Lord."** (Leviticus 23: 22-25)

Listed below are the seven feast days recorded in Leviticus 23:
1. PASSOVER
2. UNLEAVENED BREAD
3. FIRSTFRUITS
4. PENTECOST
5. TRUMPETS
6. ATONEMENT
7. TABERNACLES

The following chart lists the seven feasts as they were observed. We have included the month and number of days they were to be observed. I have also included a time line starting with the death of Christ and where that coincides with the feast days. Since the Church the Body of Christ was a mystery hid in God before the foundation of the world, it plays no part in Israel's time line, but we have shown it as a break in time. Israel is Lo-Ammi (not God's people) today., and the time for Israel will resume when the Body is raptured.

Fact: Feasts for Israel are not feasts for The Church the Body of Christ in the Dispensation of Grace.

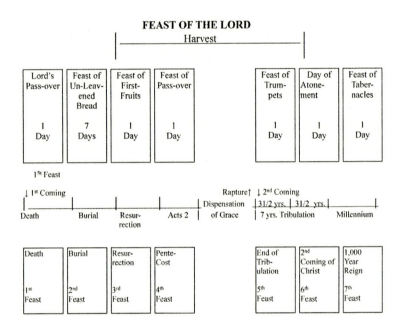

In the 21st Century, we are living in the time listed as the Dispensation of Grace. You will notice on the chart it is a period of time between Pentecost and Trumpets. Even thought the Feasts are to be observed in real time, they represent the events concerning Messiah in both real time and future time. The first four feasts have already taken place and there are three more to come, after the rapture of the Church the Body of Christ. Lets look at a brief overview of each of the feast days. (we will discuss them in detail a little later)

PASSOVER: (Leviticus 23: 4-5) This represents death, in this instance the death of Jesus. It has to do with redemption from bondage out of Egypt. The blood on the two side posts and on the upper doorpost had a two-fold purpose: identification and sanctification (Exodus 12: 1-12). Please note that the offering of blood was made by the head of the household and not by the high priest. This blood was not for the blotting out of sins; that would come on the day of the Day of Atonement. This blood was for temporal deliverance from bondage, but the atonement for sins would come at a later date.

UNLEAVENED BREAD: (Leviticus 23: 6-8) This represents the burial, of Jesus. In Matthew 16: 6, 12 this leaven is spoken of as doctrine, in this Matthew account we learn of the evil doctrine (leaven) of men. There was no evil doctrine in Jesus and therefore feeding on the *unleavened* bread of the Lord means one receives good spiritual food.

FIRSTFRUITS: (Leviticus 23: 9-14) This represents the resurrection of Jesus. It marks the beginning of the harvest (see chart) and is the feast of thanksgiving for the bountiful harvest yet to come. It is a reminder that as long as the corn is in the ground it is nothing, but it is being transformed into something new for harvest. The corn seed must die before it can be resurrected into something new.

PENTECOST: (Leviticus 23: 15-22) This represents the gathering of the crops, which in this case is souls. The Greek word "Penta" means fifty, thus the fifty days of verse 16. Israel had been sown to the world. In Acts chapter two she is being restored as God promised in Joel 2: 25-32. However, something happened and God delayed the restoration.

TRUMPETS: (Leviticus 23: 23-25) This signals the calling of Israel to Mount Zion (Isaiah 27: 12-13), in anticipation of the Lord coming back to redeem them and to blot out their sins.

ATONEMENT: (Leviticus 23: 27-32) This marks the second coming of Christ to the earth. Purpose: to redeem His people in fulfillment of His promise. The time of restitution of all things in Acts 3: 19-21 takes place at this time. Israel will be gathered back into the promise land.

TABERNACLES: (Leviticus 23: 33-44) This represents the time of the 1,000 year reign of Christ on the earth. It is from here that Christ will rule and reign with a rod of iron. During this time Satan will be bound and Israel will be safe.

GOD'S PLAN FOR THE NATION ISRAEL

When God chose Abram, it was His plan that through Abraham, Isaac and Jacob a nation would emerge – Israel. That nation's purpose was to be fruitful for the Lord and gather souls for His Kingdom.

By the time Noah, who was in the lineage Abraham, came along it was evident that the Noahtic Covenant (Genesis 11) had failed for God had scattered the people and confounded their language. Then in Genesis Chapter Twelve, God separates Abram, asking him to leave his father and his country and go to another land. Once Abram did that, showing his faith in God, the Lord promised Abram his seed (Israel) would be a blessing to the world. Abram would pass on a message to his lineage that there was one true God, and God would bless him and his seed.

Now the Lord had said unto Abram, Get thee out of thy country, and from thy kindred, and from thy father's

house, unto a land that I will shew thee: And I will make of thee a great nation, and I will bless thee, and make thy name great; and thou shalt be a blessing: And I will bless them that bless thee, and curse him that curseth thee: and in thee shall all families of the earth be blessed. (Genesis 12: 1-3)

The majority of the Old Testament deals with the promises of God to the nation Israel and the prophecy concerning them. In those Scriptures you will see documentation of Israel's failure to fulfil her obligation, how God chastises her and what He has in store for Her if she is faithful and repents. The feasts were ordained to be a reminder of her obligation and responsibility. As time transpires, Israel became a nation more concerned with the ritual and not with the purpose of the feasts, and that eventually led to her loosing favor with God.

Israel was to be a peculiar treasure, a kingdom of priest and a holy nation.

Now therefore, if ye will obey my voice indeed, and keep my covenant, then ye shall be a peculiar treasure unto me above all people: for all the earth is mine: And ye shall be unto me a kingdom of priests, and an holy nation. These are the words which thou shalt speak unto the children of Israel. (Exodus 19: 5-6)

But ye are a chosen generation, a royal priesthood, an holy nation, a peculiar people; that ye should shew forth the praises of him who hath called you out of darkness into his marvellous light: Which in time past were not a people, but are now the people of God: which had not obtained mercy, but now have obtained mercy. (1 Peter 2: 9-10)

She was chosen to represent God on earth and lead the lost to the Lord by working the fields of the world. Those of the world whom Israel harvested would then receive the blessings of Abraham. But Israel failed miserably, so God scattered them to the four winds and into the land of the Gentiles.

The Book of Hosea tells the story of fallen Israel. God instructs Hosea to take a wife of whoredoms (Gomer). Hosea is a type of Jehovah and Gomer is a type of Israel. They have three children, which represents the stages that Israel must go through. The names of the children of Hosea and Gomer are a picture of the state of Israel during their time of departure from the Lord.

JEZREEL: This was the firstborn. The name means scattering and sowing and can be found in Hosea 1: 4.

LORUHAMAH: The name means not having obtained mercy. This was the second child and the name means not having obtained mercy. (Hoses 1: 6)

LOAMMI: This was the third and last child. The name means not my people and is found in Hosea 1: 9.

So it was with Israel. God scattered her among Gentile nations and she did not learn from that so God refused to have mercy on her and allowed her to come under bondage. When God raised up Moses she reformed temporarily, but by Acts 28 she had become Loammi, not the people of God. She is still not the chosen of God today.

First she is scattered and sown. Four nations will rule over her.

That which the palmerworm hath left hath the locust eaten; and that which the locust hath left hath the cankerworm eaten; and that which the cankerworm hath left hath the caterpiller eaten. (Joel 1: 4)

The insects in the passage represent four nations:

PALMERWORM	**BABYLON**
LOCUST	**MEDIA-PERSIA**
CANKERWORM	**GREECE**
CATERPILLER	**ROME**

After being sown among Gentile nations, God has no mercy on her for a period of time with the promise to bring her back into favor.

And it shall come to pass in that day, I will hear, saith the Lord, I will hear the heavens, and they shall hear the earth; And the earth shall hear the corn, and the wine, and the oil; and they shall hear Jezreel. And I will sow her unto me in the earth; and I will have mercy upon her that had not obtained mercy; and I will say to them which were not my people, Thou art my people; and they shall say, Thou art my God. (Hosea 2: 21-23)

The third part of Israel's demise is found in Acts 28.

And when they agreed not among themselves, they departed, after that Paul had spoken one word, Well spake the Holy Ghost by Esaias the prophet unto our fathers, Saying, Go unto this people, and say, Hearing ye shall hear, and shall not understand; and seeing ye shall see, and not perceive: For the heart of this people is waxed gross, and their ears are dull of hearing, and their

eyes have they closed; lest they should see with their eyes, and hear with their ears, and understand with [their] heart, and should be converted, and I should heal them. **Be it known therefore unto you, that the salvation of God is sent unto the Gentiles, and that they will hear it.** (Acts 28: 25-28)

But God had Joel write that He would restore the people who had been declared "not my people" back to favor. **And I will restore to you the years that the locust hath eaten, the cankerworm, and the caterpiller, and the palmerworm, my great army which I sent among you.** (Joel 2: 25)

When will that be? When the restoration is complete. The start of the restoration began in Acts. The disciples were aware that restoration was to come, for they were familiar with Joel's prophecy.

And it shall come to pass afterward, that I will pour out my spirit upon all flesh; and your sons and your daughters shall prophesy, your old men shall dream dreams, your young men shall see visions: And also upon the servants and upon the handmaids in those days will I pour out my spirit. And I will shew wonders in the heavens and in the earth, blood, and fire, and pillars of smoke. The sun shall be turned into darkness, and the moon into blood, before the great and the terrible day of the Lord come. And it shall come to pass, that whosoever shall call on the name of the Lord shall be delivered: for in mount Zion and in Jerusalem shall be deliverance, as the Lord hath said, and in the remnant whom the Lord shall call. (Joel 2: 28-32)

So after Jesus was resurrected, they asked Him when that would happen. **When they therefore were come together,**

they asked of him, saying, Lord, wilt thou at this time restore again the kingdom to Israel? (Acts 1: 6) Look at Jesus' reply. **And he said unto them, It is not for you to know the times or the seasons, which the Father hath put in his own power. But ye shall receive power, after that the Holy Ghost is come upon you: and ye shall be witnesses unto me both in Jerusalem, and in all Judaea, and in Samaria, and unto the uttermost part of the earth.** (Acts 1: 7-8) The Lord did not say the time of restoration was near, nor did He say it wasn't, and then He was taken away to heaven.

Armed with this limited information the disciples make preparations to observe the Feast of Pentecost, and when the people began to speak in tongues as the Spirit gave them utterance, some questioned what was going on but Peter knew what was happening, and said: **But Peter, standing up with the eleven, lifted up his voice, and said unto them, Ye men of Judaea, and all ye that dwell at Jerusalem, be this known unto you, and hearken to my words: For these are not drunken, as ye suppose, seeing it is but the third hour of the day. But this is that which was spoken by the prophet Joel;** (Acts 2: 14-16)

Peter then quotes the prophecy of Joel 2: 28-32. Acts 2: 17-21 is the same as Joel 2: 28-32. So it is evident that Peter thought that the restoration had begun, which it had. However, it is also evident as to why the Lord could not answer that it had or had not been the time for it to begin. Why? Because it takes a downward turn in Acts 5 when Ananias and Sapphira keep back part of their possessions for themselves rather than giving them all to the disciples for equal distribution among the people.

From Acts 5 Israel begins her slide from favor to disfavor, and by Acts 28 she had completely lost favor with God and was declared Loammi. Acts 2 does not mark the beginning of the Body of Christ, it is the start of the expected restoration of Israel.

Let us explore what happened in Acts 2: 1-13.

2: 1   On the day of Pentecost, a group of Jews were gathered together and were all in one accord.
2: 2   They heard something that sounded like a mighty wind. The sound was so loud that it filled the room.
2: 3   **And there appeared unto them cloven tongues like as of fire, and it sat upon each of them.**
2: 4   **And they were all filled with the Holy Ghost, and began to speak with other tongues, as the Spirit gave them utterance.**
2: 5   The scene is Jerusalem. We find in that city devout Jews from many countries.
2: 6   These devout Jews were confounded because they heard people speaking in their native tongues.
2: 7   They were even more amazed when they discover these people were uneducated Galileans.
2: 8   They cannot seem to get over the fact they could see people talking but hearing their native tongue being spoken
2:9-11 List of all the countries from whence these devout Jews had come.
2:12   They could not figure out the meaning of all this.
2:13   That's when they determined they must be drunk with wine.

But Peter knew exactly what was happening and said: **But Peter, standing up with the eleven, lifted up his voice, and said unto them, Ye men of Judaea, and all ye that dwell**

at Jerusalem, be this known unto you, and hearken to my words: For these are not drunken, as ye suppose, seeing it is but the third hour of the day. But this is that which was spoken by the prophet Joel; (Acts 2: 14-16)

He says it is virtually impossible that these men are drunk since it is but 9: 00 am. He is certain that this is what the Prophet Joel predicted, and he proceeded to quote Joel 2: 28-32. Not only that, Peter remembered what the Lord had said prior to this day, as is found in Acts 1: 6-8.

Peter knew about the promised restoration and he knew that the events that were taking place marked the beginning of Restoration. He knew that the power Jesus said would come was here, being evidence by action of the Spirit – the Spirit of power. Let's look at what the Lord promised one more time. **But ye shall receive power, after that the Holy Ghost is come upon you: and ye shall be witnesses unto me both in Jerusalem, and in all Judaea, and in Samaria, and unto the uttermost part of the earth.** (Acts 1: 8)

What was this Spirit of power for? It was to enable them to perform miracles which should have been evidence they had favor with God and that they were God's chosen to evangelize the world. You will notice that the Lord told them they were to go to Jerusalem, all Judea, Samaria and the uttermost part of the world. Lets look at that for a moment.

Judea is the southernmost region of Israel and Jerusalem is its capital. It is also the territory of the two more faithful tribes of Israel – Judah and Benjamin.

Samaria is the capital of the northernmost region of Israel and is the home of the ten less faithful tribes.

The uttermost part of the earth may be a problem for some people since there are definitely two viewpoints. Does this mean going to all of the known world or to the parts of the world where there are Jews dwelling there after having been scattered? We believe it is the latter.

In James 1: 1 we read: **James, a servant of God and of the Lord Jesus Christ, to the twelve tribes which are scattered abroad, greeting.**

But the main reason we believe it is the latter is found in the words the Lord addresses to the disciples. **These twelve Jesus sent forth, and commanded them, saying, Go not into the way of the Gentiles, and into any city of the Samaritans enter ye not: But go rather to the lost sheep of the house of Israel.** (Matthew 10: 5-6) He also said the following in Matthew 15: 25: **But he answered and said, It is not meet to take the children's bread, and to cast it to dogs.**

In Matthew 10 Jesus tells His disciples they must not go the Gentiles, their commission is to the Jews only; and in Matthew 15 the word children means Jews and bread means the good news for the Jews. Some say that was before Christ's resurrection and now that has changed since His resurrection. Has it? Then why do you suppose Peter said: **And he said unto them, Ye know how that it is an unlawful thing for a man that is a Jew to keep company, or come unto one of another nation; but God hath shewed me that I should not call any man common or unclean.** (Acts 10: 28)

In Acts 10 we can clearly see that Peter is operating under the guidelines given Him by the Lord when He was on Earth. It is also evident that the Lord, in a vision, revealed unto Him something new. It was not that he should now go to the Gentiles but that He was preparing Peter to accept the ministry of Paul. It is the same thing he did with Ananias in Acts 9: 15: **But the Lord said unto him, Go thy way: for he is a chosen vessel unto me, to bear my name before the Gentiles, and kings, and the children of Israel:**

Paul is not an apostle to the Gentiles in Acts 2. He does not believe that Jesus is the Son of God, as Peter believed. As a matter of fact Saul (the name of Paul in the beginning) is a non-believer. In Acts 8: 1 we see that he is consenting unto the death of Stephen; and Acts 9 he has been commissioned to go to Damascus and bind believers in Christ and take them back to Jerusalem for sentencing to death.

There is no need for one to speculate as to what happened in Acts 2, one only need to believe the Scriptures. In Acts 2 Peter is addressing a group of Jews from many countries; all of whom had gather there for the purpose of observing the Jewish Feast of Pentecost..

The passages that Peter quoted from Joel was prophecy concerning Israel, looking forward to the outpouring of the Spirit of power, not the indwelling Spirit associated with the Body of Christ. The outpouring of that Spirit of power was to be the evidence of the beginning of restoration. Only part of Joel's prophecy happened in Acts 2, the rest of the prophecy will come later.

How do I know that only part of the prophecy was fulfilled in Acts two? What part do I think is future? Joel 2: 30-32: **And I will shew wonders in the heavens and in the earth, blood, and fire, and pillars of smoke. The sun shall be turned into darkness, and the moon into blood, before the great and the terrible day of the Lord come. And it shall come to pass, that whosoever shall call on the name** of the Lord shall be delivered: for in mount Zion and in Jerusalem shall be deliverance, as the Lord hath said, and in the remnant whom the Lord shall call.

And that coincides with Acts 2: 19-21: **And I will shew wonders in heaven above, and signs in the earth beneath; blood, and fire, and vapour of smoke: The sun shall be turned into darkness, and the moon into blood, before that great and notable day of the Lord come: And it shall come to pass, that whosoever shall call on the name of the Lord shall be saved.**

So what do I see in these passages that are future? Even though there have been eclipses, the sun has never gone out and the moon has never turned to blood. I also know that the day of the Lord is when He returns to earth the second time, and that event occurs after the rapture of the church.

Christ is presently seated at the right hand of the Father, far above all heavens, waiting to return and establish His earthly kingdom and the complete restoration of Israel. I know that Israel's sins have not been blotted out, and will not be until Christ returns to earth the second time. How do I know that? I believe what the Scripture says. Acts 3: 19-21:

> 19 **Repent ye therefore, and be converted, that your sins may be blotted out, when the times of refreshing shall come from the presence of the Lord;**
> 20 **And he shall send Jesus Christ, which before was preached unto you:**
> 21 **Whom the heaven must receive until the times of restitution of all things, which God hath spoken by the mouth of all his holy prophets since the world began.**

Verse 19 tells us that Israel must repent and be converted. If they do, their sins will be blotted out when the times of refreshing come – from the presence of the Lord. Verses 20 and 21 states that God will send Jesus from heaven when the restoration (times of restitution) happens, and that cannot happen until Christ returns to the earth.

In verse 19 look at the words "blotted out" carefully and compare them with the words of Acts 2: 38: **Then Peter said unto them, Repent, and be baptized every one of you in the name of Jesus Christ for the remission of sins, and ye shall receive the gift of the Holy Ghost.** The baptism for the remission of sins was a temporal thing until Jesus returns to blot them out. Sins were covered by the blood of Christ *by* the cross, not *at* the cross. But the blotting out of Israel's sins will not happen until the second coming of Christ. Don't get mad at me. If you must get mad you're going to have to get mad at the Word of God.

The times of refreshing will occur after the seven years of tribulation and at the start of the 1,000 year millennial reign of Christ. Satan is bound in the bottomless pit.

Now look at how acts 3: 21 ends: **"God hath spoken by the mouth of all his holy prophets since the world began."** All the prophets of old wrote about the events leading up to the restitution of all things. What were the prophets talking about? Isreal's sins being blotted out *at the time* of the restoration of all things. So why don't most theologians understand that? Answer: they have limited knowledge, or they have limited their knowledge so as not to make their doctrinal position invalid.

Please do not misunderstand my statement. I am not implying that I have knowledge and others do not. What I am saying is that many people have limited knowledge of Scriptural truth because they have accepted their denominational views rather than searching the Scriptures for the truth. Still others have limited their knowledge of Scripture based upon what they know to be true for the Dispensation of Grace. What they do not know is that things were different before Paul was given the message of grace. You cannot mix the things of the law with the things of grace.

Example: If you believe in eternal security you most likely believe the moment you accept Christ as Savior all your sins have been blotted out. You would be right – for today. However, that would not be right in Matthew-John and Hebrews-Revelation.

There are things in the Scripture that are excellent and things that are more excellent. There are things in the Bible that have been hid in the Scriptures and there are things that have been hid in God and revealed in the Scripture whenever God wanted it revealed. In Acts 3: 21 the fact that Israel was promised restoration on earth was written by all the prophets of old, but the mystery God revealed unto Paul concerning the Gentiles position in heaven, not on earth, were hid in God (not Scripture) before the foundation of the world.

Ephesians 1: 3-4: **Blessed be the God and Father of our Lord Jesus Christ, who hath blessed us with all spiritual blessings in heavenly places in Christ: According as he hath chosen us in him before the foundation of the world, that we should be holy and without blame before him in love:**

For this cause I Paul, the prisoner of Jesus Christ for you Gentiles, If ye have heard of the dispensation of the grace of God which is given me to you-ward: How that

by revelation he made known unto me the mystery; (as I wrote afore in few words, Whereby, when ye read, ye may understand my knowledge in the mystery of Christ) Which in other ages was not made known unto the sons of men, as it is now revealed unto his holy apostles and prophets by the Spirit; That the Gentiles should be fellowheirs, and of the same body, and partakers of his promise in Christ by the gospel: (Ephesians 3: 1-6)

And to make all men see what is the fellowship of the mystery, which from the beginning of the world hath been <u>hid in God</u>, who created all things by Jesus Christ: (Ephesians 3: 9)

Fact: Paul does not acknowledge Christ as Savior until sometime after His death, burial and resurrection.

Fact: Joel's prophecy does not mention one word about Gentiles being fellowheirs or being of the same body in Christ. You can only find that in the Pauline Epistles. Joel promised that once again Israel would be a blessing. If a Gentile was to be saved, they would be saved through the nation Israel. Ephesians 3: 6 (above) states that today Gentiles are being saved by the gospel that Paul preached. Romans 1: 16 states the gospel is the power of God unto salvation.

Fact: Israel cannot be a source of blessing today for she is Loammi, not God's people.

I believe that in the 21st century if I accept the gospel, my sins are blotted out and I am eternally secure in Christ. However, in Acts 2 & 3 that was not the case. Even though the blood of Jesus Christ was supplied for sins by what happened on Calvary, the blotting out of sins will not take place until Christ return to earth the second time, the times of restitution of all things. That is what Acts 3: 19-21 says and I believe it to be true. But Acts 3: 19-21 does not apply to believers who are saved believing the gospel committed unto Paul – the Gospel of the Grace of God.

There are too many teachers who want to mix the things of the law with the things of grace. The two do not go together anymore than oil and water do. You must learn to rightly divide the Word of Truth or you will forever be confused. Believe God's Word. If your preacher, priest, rabbi or whatever says anything contrary to the Holy Bible do not believe them. Trust God to reveal unto you the truth. But you will not receive truth apart from studying it.

If you are grounded in the Word of Truth you will be able to read any author's works and know if what they write is fact, fiction or denominational hype. The same applies if you listen to someone teach or preach. If you are grounded in truth you will know whether they are speaking the truth or telling you a fairy tale. Please quit depending totally on the words of men and start trusting in the Word of God. Learn how to study so that you may reach conclusions based upon real truth and not upon biased and preconceived ideas handed down through the ages.

WHAT HAPPENED IN ACTS TWO?

After the outpouring of the Spirit of power, not the indwelling Spirit, Peter stands and addresses a group of Jews who had gathered there for the Jewish Passover Feast.

V. 14 But Peter, standing up with the eleven, lifted up his voice, and said unto them, Ye men of Judaea, and all

ye that dwell at Jerusalem, be this known unto you, and hearken to my words:

V. 22 Ye men of Israel hear these words; Jesus of Nazareth, a man approved of God among you by miracles and wonders and signs, which God did by him in the midst of you, as ye yourselves also know:

V. 36 Therefore let all the house of Israel know assuredly, that God hath made that same Jesus, whom ye have crucified, both Lord and Christ.

He is telling his Jewish brethren that the things they are witnessing should not surprise you if you have read God's Word. The events which are transpiring on this day, were prophesied by Joel the prophet. If you are not familiar with Joel's prophecy let me tell you what was written. Joel said: **And it shall come to pass in the last days, saith God, I will pour out of my Spirit upon all flesh: and your sons and your daughters shall prophesy, and your young men shall see visions, and your old men shall dream dreams: And on my servants and on my handmaidens I will pour out in those days of my Spirit; and they shall prophesy:** (Acts 2: 17-18 is a direct quote from Joel 2: 28-29)

Peter was confident the last days were at hand. That being the case he knew that meant Christ would be returning to establish His earthly kingdom and they would be restored to the land of promise. Look at Acts 2: 39: **For the promise is unto you, and to your children, and to all that are afar off, even as many as the Lord our God shall call.** The promise was to those Jews dwelling in Jerusalem and those dwelling long distances away from Jerusalem. There is no doubt about this; Peter was addressing his fellow Jews, to whom God had promised a King and a kingdom.

Sensing they might need more proof than that of Joel, Peter quotes a passage from Psalms 110: 25-31: **For David speaketh concerning him, I foresaw the Lord always before my face, for he is on my right hand, that I should not be moved: Therefore did my heart rejoice, and my tongue was glad; moreover also my flesh shall rest in hope: Because thou wilt not leave my soul in hell, neither wilt thou suffer thine Holy One to see corruption. Thou hast made known to me the ways of life; thou shalt make me full of joy with thy countenance. Men and brethren, let me freely speak unto you of the patriarch David, that he is both dead and buried, and his sepulchre is with us unto this day. Therefore being a prophet, and knowing that God had sworn with an oath to him, that of the fruit of his loins, according to the flesh, he would raise up Christ to sit on his throne; He seeing this before spake of the resurrection of Christ, that his soul was not left in hell, neither his flesh did see corruption.**

What is Peter trying to tell them? He is saying, "In case you have misunderstood Scripture, let me enlighten you. David was not speaking about himself in the Psalms, he was telling of the future resurrection of the Messiah who is to sit on David's throne. Well brethren, part of that has happened. Messiah has come and you killed him. He has resurrected back to God, but He will return again to sit on David's throne at some future date. What is he waiting for? He is waiting for Israel to repent and be baptized."

Look at it! **This Jesus hath God raised up, whereof we all are witnesses. Therefore being by the right hand of God exalted, and having received of the Father the promise of the Holy Ghost, he hath shed forth this, which ye now see and hear. For David is not ascended into the heavens: but he saith himself, The Lord said unto my Lord, Sit thou** on my right hand, Until I make thy foes thy footstool. Therefore let all the house of Israel know assuredly, that God hath made that same Jesus, whom ye have crucified, both Lord and Christ. Now when they heard this, they were pricked in their heart, and said unto Peter and to the rest of the apostles, Men and brethren, what shall we do? Then Peter said unto them, Repent, and be baptized every one of you in the name of Jesus Christ for the remission of sins, and ye shall receive the gift of the Holy Ghost.**

This is not the preaching of a new gospel, and this is not the beginning of the Body of Christ. Peter had been teaching the same gospel since Jesus called him to be a disciple. It is the same message that John the Baptist and Jesus Himself preached. Both were calling Israel to repentance because the kingdom of heaven on earth was at hand. Once Israel repented they had to perform the required work for the time at hand – baptism.

In those days came John the Baptist, preaching in the wilderness of Judaea, And saying, Repent ye: for the kingdom of heaven is at hand. (Matthew 3: 1-2) **When John had first preached before his coming the baptism of repentance to all the people of Israel.** (Acts 13: 24) **John did baptize in the wilderness, and preach the baptism of repentance for the remission of sins.** (Mark1: 4) **From that time Jesus began to preach, and to say, Repent: for the kingdom of heaven is at hand.** (Matthew 4: 17)

IS ACTS TWO SOMETHING OLD OR SOMETHING NEW?

Have you been led to believe that in Act 2 we received a new commission to preach a new doctrine to a new group of people that will become the Church the Body of Christ? Scriptural evidence does not permit me to believe that. But the question is, "What do you believe?" Do you really think Acts 2 marks the beginning of something new or is it the realization that something promised long ago has begun? If you have read what we have presented thus far, the evidence tells you Acts 2 marks the beginning of the promised restoration of Israel into the kingdom of heaven on earth. Let's look at that evidence again.

1. Pentecost is a Jewish feast day. (Leviticus 23: 15-22)
2. It represents the beginning of the harvest for souls. (Acts 2: 41)
3. Israel was told she would be a peculiar treasure, a kingdom of priests and an holy nation, but she must keep the covenants (law) for that to happen. (Exodus 19: 3-6)
4. God scattered Israel among the Gentile nations, after a period of time having no mercy on them, eventually cutting them off from Him. However, He promised He would call them back and restore them to Himself. (Hosea 2: 21-23)
5. Joel speaks of a restoration of Israel from those who had dominion over her. (Joel 2: 25)
6. Joel also declares that once the restoration begins God would pour out His Spirit upon all flesh. (Joel 2: 28-29)
7. In Acts 2: 16 Peter says that what they are witnessing, the outpouring of the Spirit of power, is that which Joel prophesied.

So, with all this information, it is evident that Acts 2 was not the beginning of a new commission or a new gospel but the fulfillment of a long-standing promise. What happened in Acts 2-4 was the long-awaited restoration, but it soon became the beginning of the end. It was not the beginning of the Church the Body of Christ but, due to the Fall of Israel, it was the diminishing of them, which culminates in Acts 28 with their being declared "Loammi".

Here's a question for you: If Pentecost was the continuation of something old, how could the Church the Body of Christ, which is something new, have begun? It could not have! It did not! If you say it did, you may as well throw away your Bible for it will be of no use to you.

THE FEAST DAYS DETAILED

The First Passover: (Exodus 12: 2-12) God instructed the head of the household to put blood all around the door. What was the purpose? So that when the death angel came he would pass over that house and the firstborn male within the house would have his life spared.

Note: The blood was not for remission of sins even though the feast is representative of the death of Jesus. Why? Because it was the head of the household who administered the blood on the door, the High Priest must administer blood from the sacrificial lamb in order to obtain remission of sins. Israel's deliverance was from bondage, not sin; deliverance from sins takes place on the Day of Atonement.

Jesus observing the Passover meal with the twelve: What was that all about? He told the disciples that as often as they ate or drank the Passover Meal they should remember Him, or as 1 Corinthians 11: 26 states, remember his death until He comes back. In other words Christ was preparing them for the time He would come back to blot out their sins.

Members of the Body of Christ have their sins blotted out the moment they believe. They *do not* have to wait for Christ to return for that to happen, but Peter, the twelve and those saved under the gospel of the circumcision *do* have to wait.

FEAST OF PASSOVER: Passover began on the 14th day of the first month, at evening (probably 14 days after the Spring equinox). It represents the death of Christ and deliverance from bondage. But just as the blood over the door and on the side post did not atone for Israel's sins at the time the angel of death passed over them in Egypt, neither did the blood shed by the Lord on Calvary atone for Israel's sin at that moment in time. We will see that happening on the Day of Atonement. Just as the blood over the door and on the side post was necessary for deliverance from bondage, so too, the blood at Calvary was necessary for remission of sins awaiting the time when their sins would be atoned for-- three feast days later.

Do not be confused. What we have today is different from what the saved had before the time of the Lord's first coming and even after His death, burial and resurrection. Israel will have their sins blotted out (atoned for) when the Lord returns to earth the second time. Our sins were blotted out (atoned for) the moment we believed. If you do not rightly divided the Scriptures you will have limited your ability to have a clearer understanding of the Word of God.

FACT: The blood for remission of sins was provided for everybody by what happened at Calvary; but Israel's atonement for sins did not take place AT Calvary – that is future.

The Passover Feast represents the death of Jesus but the Feast of Atonement is not observed until there have been three other feasts: Firstfruits, Pentecost and Trumpets. Look at the following two verses with an open mind and without limiting yourself.

Then Peter said unto them, Repent, and be baptized every one of you in the name of Jesus Christ for the remission of sins, and ye shall receive the gift of the Holy Ghost. (Acts 2: 38)

Repent ye therefore, and be converted, that your sins may be blotted out, when the times of refreshing shall come from the presence of the Lord; (Acts 3: 19)

The passages are clear. Israel sins will not be blotted out until Christ's 2nd coming.

FEAST OF UNLEAVENED BREAD: This feast began one day after the Feast of Passover, on the 15th. It was also observed on the Sabbath. In John 19: 31 the Jews sought to have the Lord's body taken down from the cross to be buried before the Sabbath, which also happened to be the day of observance for the Feast of Unleavened Bread.

This feast represents the burial of Jesus Christ. "Unleavened" is symbolic of purity and represents the body of the Lord Jesus. As you read your Bible, you will find numerous passages of Scripture describing Christ as "The Bread of Life." As you study, you will understand that the Scriptures are the true, pure words of God. Feed on them and not on the words of men. Be aware that all who preach or teach the Bible do not necessarily preach the truth contained in the Bible. These people seem to have their own agenda and if the Bible conflicts with their denominational views or creed they allow those things to take precedence over the Word of God.

FEAST OF FIRSTFRUITS: This feast day represents the resurrection of Jesus and was observed eight days after the start of the Feast of Unleavened Bread. The number eight is seven (the number of perfection) plus one (the beginning); it is the number associated with resurrection, regeneration and the beginning of a new era. Eight souls went through the flood, Noah, his three sons and the wives of each. Christ's grave was found empty on the first day of the week (John 20: 10) and He is the firstfruits of the dead.

For as in Adam all die, even so in Christ shall all be made alive. But every man in his own order: Christ the firstfruits; afterward they that are Christ's at his coming. (1 Corinthians 15: 22-23)

It is no coincidence that Christ was not in the grave on the day the Feast of Firstfruits began, which was a Sunday. That is the reason Christians observe the first day of the week rather than the Sabbath, which is a Saturday. That is why we, who are saved under grace, are to forget about ordinances of the law and of the things that were of an earthly nature. **Wherefore henceforth know we no man after the flesh: yea, though we have known Christ after the flesh, yet now henceforth know we him no more. (2 Corinthians 5: 16)**

The feast days were important for Israel; they need to be understood by Gentiles in order to have a clearer understanding and appreciation of what we have under grace. The Feast of Firstfruits marks the beginning of the harvest; in this case it is the harvest of souls. It does not mark the beginning of a new body, but it marks the beginning of the restoration of Israel. Israel, who had gone a whoring from God, was to begin to lead souls to the knowledge that Messiah had come and would soon establish His earthly kingdom.

FEAST OF PENTECOST: This is the beginning of the gathering of the harvest (Israel); it begins with the first 3,000 souls being saved in Acts 2: 41: **Then they that gladly received his word were baptized: and the same day there were added unto them about three thousand souls.** The restoration of Israel began at this point in time, but it did not last very long for the restoration is now in abeyance because Israel is Loammi.

The following passage is often times a confrontational point, as there are many opinions about it. Leviticus 23: 17: **Ye shall bring out of your habitations two wave loaves of two tenth deals: they shall be of fine flour; they shall be baken with leaven; they are the firstfruits unto the Lord.**

There are those that say the two loaves typify Christ, but I say that it cannot because: 1) They are made with leaven, and we have already stated that leaven is associated with evil doctrine; 2) They are the firstfruits, but we have already read the Christ was the firstfruits.

God knew Israel would become divided into two groups: 1) The two faithful tribes, and, 2) The ten unfaithful tribes. The two leavened loaves was for each of these groups. God is saying, even though you have become separated, I will make you one again, as we see written in Ezekiel 37: 22: **And I will make them one nation in the land upon the mountains of Israel; and one king shall be king to them all: and they shall be no more two nations, neither shall they be divided into two kingdoms any more at all:**

The confusion about the two loaves is carried even further by some. For they say the two loaves represent Israel and Gentiles; which is yet another effort to justify their belief that the Body of Christ began with Pentecost in Acts two.

I will not even attempt to give you their explanation of the verse above for they are so ludicrous. If they would read verse 21 it would be clear: **And say unto them, Thus saith the Lord GOD; Behold, I will take the children of Israel from among the heathen, whither they be gone, and will gather them on every side, and bring them into their own land:** Do not let someone quote you one verse without looking at several verses before it and after it.

Ezekiel's prophecy was happening in Acts 2. The children of Israel were all in one accord and had become one nation again. **And they, continuing daily with <u>one accord</u> in the temple, and breaking bread from house to house, did eat their meat with gladness and singleness of heart,** (Acts 2: 46). It is clear isn't it? So why do denominations not see it? Could it not be pride or prejudice?

I can tell you something about pride. When I was first introduced to rightly dividing the truth I tried to find fault with it. Even when I saw the truth of it, I refused to acknowledge it as being truth. "How can so many Baptists be wrong," I said. "I have been teaching the Baptist belief that the Body of Christ began in Acts 2. What are those people going to think about me if I tell them I was wrong?" Pride, it was the downfall of Lucifer and it was beginning to be mine. It was hard to leave the life I had known for so long; but I had to because it was the wrong life. When we refuse to believe the Word of Truth we do not enjoy a perfect life with Christ. The teaching of men will rob you of that joy if their teaching is not based upon the truth, rightly divided.

There are too many people who are looking for that calm assurance they believe should follow salvation, when it does not come as quickly as they think it should, they turn to self gratifying experiences that do nothing more than edify self.

He that speaketh in an unknown tongue edifieth himself; but he that prophesieth edifieth the church. (1 Corinthians 14: 4)

After the tongues experience ceases to satisfy your need, try studying the Truth rightly divided. You will never get tired of it for it is of God and not of self. Only God can give us peace within. Oh yes, there will still be mountains and valleys you will have to go through here on earth, but the hope that lies ahead for us in heaven is worth all we must endure. Unlike men, God's Word does not contradict itself. If you think it does, it could be because you have limited your knowledge of Scripture by believing what your ears have heard and not what your soul knew to be true.

If we see that Pentecost marks the beginning of the restoration of Israel, we can also see the necessity of Matthias being appointed as the twelfth apostle. This is lost when we try to make Acts 2 the beginning of the body, for there must be twelve apostles in the New Jerusalem. **And the wall of the city had twelve foundations, and in them the names of the twelve apostles of the Lamb.** (Revelation 21: 14) Paul could not be the twelfth apostle, as many people believe, for his home is far above all heavens.

FEAST OF TRUMPETS: This is the calling of Israel together to wait for the Lord's 2nd return to earth. So the trumpet sounds to announce His coming. The trumpet is a common instrument used throughout the Bible: **1)** It was used to proclaim liberty in the year of Jubilee (Leviticus 25: 8-10); **2)** We see in connection with the Feast of Trumpets in Leviticus 23: 24 and ; **3)** 1 Corinthians 15: 52 it is used when discussing resurrection. The trumpet was used in connection with judgment and liberty; judgment being necessary before liberty could be proclaimed.

FEAST OF ATONEMENT: Of all the feasts, this one is most important for it is the feast when Israel's sins will be completely blotted out. **Repent ye therefore, and be converted, that your sins may be blotted out, when the times of refreshing shall come from the presence of the Lord;** (Acts 3: 19)

Okay, let's see what has transpired: **1)** We had the Feast of Passover, which represented the death of the Lord; **2)** Then we had the Feast of Unleavened Bread which represented the burial of Jesus; **3)** The Feast of Firstfruits represented the resurrection of the Lord. Then we came to **4)** The Feast of Pentecost, which, we said, marked the beginning of the Harvest. In Acts two the disciples began harvesting souls, anticipating the restoration of Israel. After Pentecost we come to **5)** The Feast of Trumpets which is to announce the 2nd coming of the Lord and which ends the harvesting for souls; for the time has come for the kingdom to be established, and that happens with the **6)** Feast of Atonement and the Lord's physical return to earth.

Let us be clear, the blood for the remission of sins was provided **by** what happened on Calvary, i.e. Feast of Passover and the death of Jesus Christ. However, Israel's sins would not be blotted out until the Feast of Atonement, which represents the 2nd coming of Christ.

If this is confusing to you it is probably because you have knowledge of what is promised us under the gospel of the uncircumcision (grace/Paul's Gospel), which is different from what Israel had been promised under the gospel of the circumcision (Peter's Gospel). The blood of Jesus Christ was shed for both groups of people, but one group receives the benefits of it before the other one does.

Those who teach that baptism is necessary for repentance to those of us under grace err because they do not understand that Pentecost was a Jewish feast day for remission of sins, but those sins would not be blotted out until the Feast of Atonement. Our sins were blotted out the moment we believed. So you can see why it is necessary to understand the feasts days in order to rightly divide that which was for Israel and that which is for us.

Once Christ was resurrected we see Peter with a group of about 120 people gathered together in an upper room. What were they there for? They were waiting for the Spirit of power to come, which would be instrumental in their harvesting lost souls before the 2nd coming of Christ.

Look closely at Acts 1: 1-2: **The former treatise have I made, O Theophilus, of all that Jesus began both to do and teach, Until the day in which he was taken up, after that he through the Holy Ghost had given commandments unto the apostles whom he had chosen:**

What did Jesus teach His disciples? Let's look and see.

1) **These twelve Jesus sent forth, and commanded them, saying, Go not into the way of the Gentiles, and into any city of the Samaritans enter ye not:** (Matthew 10: 5-6) Is it not clear the disciples were to go to Jews and not Gentiles?
2) When the woman from Canaan (a Gentile) asked for mercy from the Lord, what did he tell her? **But he answered and said, I am not sent but unto the lost sheep of the house of Israel.** (Matthew 15: 24) Fact: Jesus was sent to Israel.
3) Jesus knew that water baptism was a temporal act representing the remission of sins, therefore John the

Baptist was ordained of God to announce this new requirement. **And he came into all the country about Jordan, preaching the baptism of repentance for the remission of sins;** (Luke 3: 3) That is why Peter said what he did in Acts 2: 38: **Then Peter said unto them, Repent, and be baptized every one of you in the name of Jesus Christ for the remission of sins, and ye shall receive the gift of the Holy Ghost.**

4) What would happen if they repented and were baptized? They would receive the gift of the Holy Ghost.
5) And what was the next order of the day for Israel? Their sins would be blotted out. Acts 3: 19: **Repent ye therefore, and be converted, that your sins may be blotted out, when the times of refreshing shall come from the presence of the Lord;**
6) When would the blotting out of sins take place? When the times of refreshing shall come, and that happens at the 2nd coming of Christ. (Acts 3: 19)
7) Where is Jesus Christ now? In heaven, and Acts 3: 21 states that He must be received in Heaven before and until He will return to earth. (Acts 3:20-21)

If you will take the time to study the Scriptures you will see what has been presented is truth, and you would know that the blotting out of sins for Israel and the Body of Christ do not occur at the same time. Those who want to start the Body of Christ at Acts 2 have missed the purpose of the Feast days. They were for Israel. They were a picture of that which was to come. And they would culminate with the last feast day – the millennial reign of Christ.

FEAST OF TABERNACLES: This feast is all about the millennial reign of Christ, or as it is more commonly known, the 1,000 year reign of Christ. (Revelation 20: 4) The Jew is waiting for the day when God will restore them into the land of promise. Why? Because they know that at that time Messiah will reign as King over the earth.. This period of time is not the final kingdom of God, which comes after Satan has been cast into the lake of fire.

Are there differences of opinion concerning Acts two?

Yes, there are several opinions about this verse.

1. Some say this is where the Church the Body of Christ began and the speaking in tongues and the prophesying are things we should be doing today.
2. Some say this is where the Church the Body of Christ began but tongues and prophesying are not things we should be doing today.
3. Some say that baptism is necessary for salvation.
4. Some say that baptism is not necessary for salvation.
    a. Some of these say the "Repent and be baptized for the remission of sins" means: get baptized with the understanding you already have remission of sins.
    b. Others say baptism was a part of the law and is not valid under grace for salvation.
5. Some say Acts 2 is for Jews only.
6. Some say Acts 2 is for Jews and Gentiles.

So, whom do you believe? Do you believe the teacher who is the most eloquent speaker? Do you believe the person who is more passionate? Do you believe the individual who is the kindest? None of these should be the determining factor in choosing what is right. The only sensible thing to believe is the Word of God, not what someone said the word of God said. Make sure you have a Bible that is not tainted by men. My recommendation is that you get a King James Bible. There are many translations, but I have found a King James Bible to be the most reliable.

Baptism – the most divisive subject in Christendom.

Baptism In the Old Testament

The word *baptize* is found twice in: 1) 2 Kings 5: 14, used of Nathan when he "dipped" himself in the Jordan River; 2) Isaiah 21: 4.

Bapto is found 18 times, nine of them in the Law of Moses where it is used of *dipping* in blood, oil or in water.

Baptos is found only one time in Ezekiel 23: 15.

In the New Testament there are three references to Old Testament baptism: 1) The Ark and the Flood (1 Peter 3: 21)' 2) Crossing of the Red Sea (1 Corinthians 10: 2) and, 3) Carnal ordinances of the Tabernacle (Hebrews 9: 10).

Baptism In the New Testament

The teaching of baptism is broken into the following categories:
1. John the Baptist.
    a. It was a baptism unto repentance, looking forward to atonement prior to entry into the kingdom. (Matthew 3: 1-2)
    b. It concerned Israel.
    c. It was a baptism of water that spoke of a future baptism with fire and the Holy Ghost.

2. The baptism with the Holy Ghost, as promised by John, was fulfilled at Pentecost (Acts 1: 5).
3. During the Acts period, water baptism and baptism of the Spirit went together. (Acts 2: 38; 10: 37)
4. Practiced by Paul during his early ministry (1 Corinthians 1: 16), but baptism was not a part of his gospel for salvation. (1 Corinthians 1: 17) It was an important part of Peter's gospel. Peter could not say, "Christ sent me not to baptize".
5. In the Prison Epistles of Paul water baptism gave way to spiritual baptism.

Baptism in the Pauline Epistles

Paul's Epistles are divided into two segments: Pre-prison and Prison/Post Prison.

Pre-prison: These are Epistles written prior to Paul being confined to a Roman prison. They are: Romans, 1 Corinthians, 2 Corinthians, Galatians, 1 Thessalonians and 2 Thessalonians. We often refer to these books as the works of Paul's early ministry. You will find that in these Epistles Paul is "all things to all men." (1 Corinthians 9: 19-23) He did a lot of things early on that he ceased doing after receiving revelations from the Lord to stop.

Prison/Post Prison: These Epistles are: Ephesians, Philippians, Colossians, 1 Timothy, 2 Timothy, Titus and Philemon. In teaching, we often refer to the Epistles as relating to his later ministry. As you read these books you will see that ordinances practiced early on became stumbling blocks. In these seven books Paul no longer tries to be all things to all people. Why? Because Israel has become Loammi and the ordinances the church were to keep have been set aside.

The one baptism of Ephesians 4: 5 is spiritual baptism, not water baptism.

Acts: Battleground of Dispensational Truth.

For the most part, Acts is about the ministries of Peter and Paul. Peter dominates the first 12 chapters before being supplanted by James, the brother of Jesus. Paul is seen as Saul in Acts 8; he is converted in Acts 9 and his missionary journeys begin in Acts 13 and culminate in Acts 28.

Galatians 2: 7: **But contrariwise, when they saw that the gospel of the uncircumcision was committed unto me, as the gospel of the circumcision was unto Peter**. Paul speaks of the gospel committed unto him and the gospel committed unto Peter. He clarifies that by stating his was the gospel of the uncircumcision and Peter's was the gospel of the circumcision. In 2 Timothy 1: 11 Paul is called the apostle of the Gentiles. If you can see that Paul and Peter have separate callings you will be better prepared to understand what transpires in Acts.

Acts 2 is not about the Body of Christ, but about Israel. As you proceed through the chapters you will begin to see that the Book of Acts is all about Israel's decline, and finally being declared Loammi in Acts 28. While there is Body truth in Acts, the Book focuses on Isreal's decline.

The Three Major Divisions in Acts

	Acts 1-12	**Acts 13-16**	**Acts 17-28**
City	Jerusalem	Antioch	Rome
Figure	Peter	Paul & Others	Paul
People	Jews Primarily	Jews & Gentiles	Gentiles Primarily
Gospel Preached	*Gospel of God	*Gospel of Christ	*Gospel of the Grace of God
Message For The Jews	Beginning Of Restoration	Gentile Reconciliation	Loammi Rejection

* I am not saying there were three separate Gospels, what I am saying is that the teaching of Jesus Christ changes as Paul is given Divine revelations. For instance:

The Gospel of God is simply teaching that Jesus is the Son of God. Peter and Paul both preach this.

The Gospel of Christ teaches Jesus, the Son of God, died for your sins. Peter and Paul both taught this, but Peter taught that sins would be blotted out when Christ returned the 2nd time; Paul taught sins were blotted out the moment one trusted Christ as Savior.

The Gospel of the Grace of God teaches Jesus, the Son of God, died for your sins, even those Gentiles who were without hope. (Eph. 2: 11-13) Paul taught this and Peter never preached it.

Restoration For Israel Started In Acts

If you read the Book of Isaiah you will find that it is divided into two major sections. The first 39 chapters pertain to the rejection of Israel and chapters 40-66 pertain to the restoration of Israel. Isaiah 40: 1-3:

Comfort ye, comfort ye my people, saith your God. Speak ye comfortably to Jerusalem, and cry unto her, that her warfare (appointed time) **is accomplished, that her iniquity is pardoned: for she hath received of the Lord's hand double for all her sins. <u>The voice of him that crieth in the wilderness,</u> Prepare ye the way of the Lord, make straight in the desert a highway for our God.** The Hebrew word for warfare is *tsaba'* and in Daniel 10: 1 that word is translated as time appointed.

What I hope you see here is that the prophecy of Isaiah speaks of an appointed time when Israel's iniquities will be accomplished. Isaiah is prophesying about restoration. I underlined

"The voice of him crying in the desert" because this makes reference to John the Baptist, who announced the coming of the Messiah, without whom there could be no restoration.

Peter had a clear understanding of the prophecy of Daniel, Isaiah, Malachi, Hosea and Joel, that is why he was sure that what was transpiring in Acts 2 was in fulfillment of Joel's prophecy concerning the restoration of Israel. (Joel 2: 25-32)

In Malachi 4: 5 we read: **Behold, I will send you Elijah the prophet before the coming of the great and dreadful day of the Lord:** Perhaps that prophecy also came to mind after Jesus spoke theses words: **For all the prophets and the law prophesied until John. And if ye will receive it, this is Elias** (Elijah), **which was for to come**. However, Israel did not receive it and Elijah must come at some point in the future. That will happen at some point during the seven years of tribulation.

Can you not see that what transpired in Acts 2 was a partial fulfillment of prophecy? Organized religion may not see this, but the apostles did. **Which also said, Ye men of Galilee, why stand ye gazing up into heaven? this same Jesus, which is taken up from you into heaven, shall so come in like manner as ye have seen him go into heaven.** (Acts 1: 11) These words were spoken to them by angels, which perhaps brought to mind this passage from Zechariah 14: 4: **And his feet shall stand in that day upon the mount of Olives, which is before Jerusalem on the east, and the mount of Olives shall cleave in the midst thereof toward the east and toward the west, and there shall be a very great valley; and half of the mountain shall remove toward the north, and half of it toward the south.**

With the words of the angels ringing in their ears and the prophetic passages hidden in their hearts, the Apostles must have been chomping at the bits over the prospect that fulfillment of the promised restoration was at hand. So, the Apostles got down to business and elected someone to take the place of Judas; for they knew that, in the regeneration, twelve thrones must be occupied by twelve Apostles. They elected Mathias.

With everything in order, they were almost ready, but one more thing had to happen before restoration could begin – the power to go forth and reach Jews everywhere. They were waiting for the Holy Ghost of power to descend upon them, and it did on the day of Pentecost. Israel had been a rebellious nation but this day marked a dramatic change in her; but sadly the change was short lived. The harvest began with many souls turning to God, but almost as quickly as it came so came the demise. Several thousand repented and were baptized but hundreds of thousands did not. Israel failed one more time, and before too long God would say He had enough of Her and she was declared Loammi.

God knew this would happen, for Scripture tells us He had made preparations for this event before the foundation of the world, before the calling of Abraham. God chose to raise up the Gentiles to carry on where Israel had failed. "**According as he hath chosen us in him before the foundation of the world, that we should be holy and without blame before him in love:**" Ephesians 1: 4.

Reconciliation

The Apostle Paul was chosen to lead these Gentiles into a far greater commission than that which Jesus gave his disciples. (Matthew 28: 19-20) That commission is known as the ministry of reconciliation. Paul had been chosen for this task long before he believed Jesus was Messiah. **But when it pleased God, who separated me from my mother's womb, and called me by his grace, To reveal his Son in me, that I might preach him among the heathen; immediately I conferred not with flesh and blood:** (Galatians 1: 15-16)

But the religious leaders of the Jews refused to acknowledge Paul's apostleship. They went to great lengths to discredit his authority and the message he preached. People in the 21st century do the same thing. Too many religions refuse to believe the uniqueness of the complete message of Paul, but they will take some of it (the liberty it preaches) and discard most of it as being nothing significant.

Our Greater Commission - The ministry of Reconciliation:

And all things are of God, who hath reconciled us to himself by Jesus Christ, and hath given to us the ministry of reconciliation; To wit, that God was in Christ, reconciling the world unto himself, not imputing their trespasses unto them; and hath committed unto us the word of reconciliation. Now then we are ambassadors for Christ, as though God did beseech you by us: we pray you in Christ's stead, be ye reconciled to God. For he hath made him to be sin for us, who knew no sin; that we might be made the righteousness of God in him. 2 Corinthians 5: 18-21)

Under the ministry of Paul the Gentile comes to a place of prominence and blessing. At a certain point in time we cease to read the words "Jews Only" or "Ye men of Israel." As a matter of fact, God in His wisdom had to bring Israel down in order that the Gentiles could be raised up. "**What then? Israel hath not obtained that which he seeketh for; but** the election hath obtained it, and the rest were blinded What then? Israel hath not obtained that which he seeketh for; but the election hath obtained it, and the rest were blinded And David saith, Let their table be made a snare, and a trap, and a stumblingblock, and a recompence unto them: Let their eyes be darkened, that they may not see, and bow down their back alway. I say then, Have they stumbled that they should fall? God forbid: but rather through their fall salvation is come unto the Gentiles, for to provoke them to jealousy."** (Romans 11: 7-11)

Paul is the only apostle to use the word reconciliation for he is the APOSTLE TO THE GENTILES.

THE BEGINNING OF THE CHURCH
THE BODY OF CHRIST

Before we analyze the subject it is necessary to define a few words.

Definition # 1 - CHURCH

The Greek word for church is *ekklesia* and has been translated in English as *ecclesia* and is defined as: a gathering of citizens called out from their homes into some public place, an assembly. In the Old Testament the Greek word ekklesia is used to translate the Hebrew word *qahal,* which means to call or to assemble. It is from this verb form that we get the noun congregation or assembly.

In Acts 7: 38, Stephen referred to Moses' leadership and the history of Israel: **This is he, that was in the CHURCH in the wilderness with the angel which spake to him in the mount Sina, and with our fathers: who received the lively**

oracles to give unto us: Israel was the church of that period, she was called out of Egypt and assembled together under the leadership of Moses.

You need to understand that the word ekklesia (church) does not always mean a gathering or an assembly of God-fearing people. We can see that in Acts19.

Verse 32: **Some therefore cried one thing, and some another: for the assembly** (ekklesia) **was confused; and the more part knew not wherefore they were come together.**
Verse 39: **But if ye enquire any thing concerning other matters, it shall be determined in a lawful assembly.**
Verse 41: **And when he had thus spoken, he dismissed the assembly** (ekklesia).

There was a church before Pentecost. Look at Matthew 18: 17: **And if he shall neglect to hear them, tell it unto the <u>church</u>: but if he neglect to hear the <u>church</u>, let him be unto thee as an heathen man and a publican.**

So if you say the church began at Pentecost, shouldn't you ask what church? Was it:

1. The church in the wilderness? (Acts 7: 38)
2. The church of Christ's early ministry and before Pentecost? (Matthew 18: 17)
3. The future church spoken of? (Matthew 16: 18)
4. The seven churches of Asia as found in Revelation chapters 1-3? It is interesting that one of those churches is at Pergamos, which will be the city "where Satan's seat is". (Revelation 2:13)
5. The Church the Body of Christ? (Ephesians 1: 22-23)

Interestingly enough, the first four churches above speak of an assembly of people, whether saved or lost. But the church mentioned in number five speaks of those who are a part of Christ's body. The first four are physical and number five is spiritual. The Church the Body of Christ is a living organism with Christ as its head. The other churches mentioned are but a group of people assembled together on earth.

Definition # 2 – BODY

The English word "body" is translated from the Greek word *soma*. In almost all cases it refers to the actual physical body. In Corinthians, Ephesians and Colossians it is used of believers which are made part of Christ's body by spiritual baptism. **For by one Spirit are we all baptized into one body, whether we be Jews or Gentiles, whether we be bond or free; and have been all made to drink into one Spirit.** (1 Corinthians 12: 13)

Ephesians 1: 22-23: **And hath put all things under his feet, and gave him to be the head over all things to the church, which is his body, the fulness of him that filleth all in all**. We see here that Christ is the head of this particular body. Col.2:19: **And not holding the Head, from which all the body by joints and bands having nourishment ministered, and knit together, increaseth with the increase of God.** The two (body and Head) are inseparable and this Church will be exalted with Christ, as seen in Ephesians 2: 6: **And hath raised us up together, and made us sit together in heavenly places in Christ Jesus:**

It is interesting that the Church the Body of Christ is the fullness of Christ. The thought is that without this group of believers, this Church, Christ is not or will not be complete. It is also interesting that Paul is the only apostle who preached of this church. Why do you suppose that is true? Because the church that Peter and the other apostles spoke of will be physically situated on the earth, not far above all heavens.

Definition # 3 – The Church the Body of Christ

The Church the Body of Christ is a called-out group of people who are joined to Christ by spiritual baptism and is seated together with Christ in heavenly places. Christ is the head of this church. Members will make Christ complete, therefore equal with Him.

Definition # 4 – The Church that began at Pentecost

Is a called-out group of people who will be gathered together on the earth at the 2nd coming of Christ. Christ will be its King. Members of this church will not be a part of Christ's body, they will be subservient to Him, for He will rule them with a rod of iron.

Three viewpoints concerning the beginning of the Church the Body of Christ.

Acts 2: Those who take this position say the outpouring of the Holy Ghost was indication of a change, therefore a new beginning. They are of the opinion that the Spirit that came down was the indwelling Spirit.

Mid-Acts: Those who take this position believe the Church the Body of Christ could not have begun before the salvation of Paul, who is the Apostle of the uncircumcision and the only one who speaks specifically about the Body. Paul is not saved until Acts 9 and begins his missionary work in Acts 13.

Acts 28: Those who take this position believe in the unique ministry of Paul but believe the body could not have begun before Israel became Loammi, which happens in Acts 28. They acknowledge a body of believers in mid-Acts who have a heavenly inheritance, but not far above all heavens. They propose a split body.

So, how can one know which viewpoint is the real one? You will find it by studying. We have already given you sufficient information as to why it could not have begun in Acts 2 because that was not the start of something new, it was the continuation of something old. However, you need to understand that the majority of professing Christians do take this position. That does not necessarily mean they are right. The religious leaders of Jesus' day wanted Him crucified. **But Pilate answered them, saying, Will ye that I release unto you the King of the Jews? For he knew that the chief priests had delivered him for envy. But the chief priests moved the people, that he should rather release Barabbas unto them. And Pilate answered and said again unto them, What will ye then that I shall do unto him whom ye call the King of the Jews? And they cried out again, Crucify him.** (Mark 15: 9-13)

It takes little courage to follow the majority but it takes great courage to stand for the truth when so many oppose it. In Acts 6 & 7 Stephen was preaching in the power of the Spirit and drew unfavorable comments from the Jews, (6: 9) who stirred up the people against him.(6: 12) He doesn't pay any attention to their ridicule, but uses the occasion to preach truth unto them. Though he was only one against many, he preached the truth until they gnashed on him with their teeth. (7: 54) All he could see was the Son of Man standing at the right hand of the Father, (7: 56). When he told the crowd that, they cried out and stopped their ears (7: 57) and then overpowered him and stoned him to death (7: 58-60). For Stephen, the truth was more important than opposition, even if it meant death. Is truth important to you?

Saul: The opposition leader

The first mention of Saul is found in Acts chapter seven. The witnesses of the stoning of Stephen laid down their clothes at the feet of Saul, who in Acts 8 consented (approved) unto his death. Saul was one of the most villainous of the Christian haters. Look at Acts 8:3: **As for Saul, he made havock of the church, entering into every house, and haling men and women committed them to prison.**

In the beginning of Acts 9 you will find more evidence of Saul's passion against the followers of Jesus. He presents himself before the High Priest and asks for authority to seek out these people, intent on having them brought back to Jerusalem for execution. This is how Paul described himself after he was saved. **Which thing I also did in Jerusalem: and many of the saints did I shut up in prison, having received authority from the chief priests; and when they were put to death, I gave my voice against them. And I punished them oft in every synagogue, and compelled them to blaspheme; and being exceedingly mad against them, I persecuted them even unto strange cities.** (Acts 26: 10-11)

Saul was a zealot for the traditions of the Jews and was very vocal against those who questioned the veracity of the Jewish religion. Look at his own words in Galatians 1: 13-14: **For ye have heard of my conversation in time past in the Jews' religion, how that beyond measure I persecuted the church of God, and wasted it: And profited in the Jews' religion above many my equals in mine own nation,**

being more exceedingly zealous of the traditions of my fathers. You can see that being zealous for a cause may not be a good thing. As a matter of fact Paul said as much in his letter to the Romans. **Brethren, my heart's desire and prayer to God for Israel is, that they might be saved. For I bear them record that they have a zeal of God, but not according to knowledge.** (Romans 10: 1-2)

There are far too many zealots for God who do not have the knowledge of Pauline truth. Saul, the zealot for the law, became Paul, the zealot for Christ. But Paul spent many days and nights in one-on-one conversations with the Lord. As you read the Scriptures you will see that Paul had many revelations from the Lord concerning his job and the words he would teach. Some of those revelations had been hidden in Old Testament Scripture, others had been hidden in God.

How much do you know about the mystery revealed unto Paul? How much do you know about Paul, period? Did you know that apart from the Pauline epistle you would never find salvation by grace? Too many professing Christians want to enjoy the liberty of grace but insist upon practicing the restrictions of the law. Is there any wonder why there is so much confusion in the churches today?

Saul: Confronted by Jesus

Saul left for Damascus with letters of authority against the followers of Christ, but he never presented those papers to the priests at Damascus. Before reaching his destination he was blinded by the light of God and heard the voice of God: **And he fell to the earth, and heard a voice saying unto him, Saul, Saul, why persecutest thou me? And he said, Who art thou, Lord? And the Lord said, I am Jesus whom thou persecutest: it is hard for thee to kick against**

the pricks. And he trembling and astonished said, Lord, what wilt thou have me to do? And the Lord said unto him, Arise, and go into the city, and it shall be told thee what thou must do. (Acts 9: 4-6)

Saul, the persecutor of Christians, had met the God-Man, Jesus Christ, whom he opposed. He didn't ask who He was; Saul knew it was the Lord talking. He was never the same again. Neither will you be, if you have truly met the Savior face-to-face. Perhaps you are one of those people that discredit Paul's teaching. Are you truly a child of God? You cannot be if you do not believe the Gospel committed unto Paul. Why not trust Christ right now? He will save you if you accept what He did, died for your sins, was buried and raised up for your justification.

The Lord did not tell Saul that things were going to be easy from that point on; He told Ananias he was going to have to suffer. **But the Lord said unto him, Go thy way: for he is a chosen vessel unto me, to bear my name before the Gentiles, and kings, and the children of Israel: For I will shew him how great things he must suffer for my name's sake.** (Acts 9: 15-16)

And suffer he did. He constantly had to defend his apostleship and the message revealed to him to preach. Denominationalists look upon preachers of Pauline truth as though they were a cult. But it doesn't matter what they think, the Jewish leaders thought the same thing, but Paul persevered and so must we. Our job, like Paul's, is: **And to make all men see what is the fellowship of the mystery, which from the beginning of the world hath been hid in God, who created all things by Jesus Christ:** (Ephesians 3: 9)

Paul's Apostleship

He was not the twelfth apostle, as some suppose; but he was an apostle chosen of God. **And that he was seen of Cephas, then of the twelve: After that, he was seen of above five hundred brethren at once; of whom the greater part remain unto this present, but some are fallen asleep. After that, he was seen of James; then of all the apostles. And last of all he was seen of me also, as of one born out of due time.** (1 Corinthians 15: 5-8)

This apostle, chosen of God, was given a message which was different from the message God had given the twelve. **But contrariwise, when they saw that the gospel of the uncircumcision was committed unto me, as the gospel of the circumcision was unto Peter; (For he that wrought effectually in Peter to the apostleship of the circumcision, the same was mighty in me toward the Gentiles:) And when James, Cephas, and John, who seemed to be pillars, perceived the grace that was given unto me, they gave to me and Barnabas the right hands of fellowship; that we should go unto the heathen, and they unto the circumcision.** The twelve were called during Christ's earthly ministry and Paul was called after the death, burial and resurrection of the Lord.

Paul: Sent to the Gentiles

For I speak to you Gentiles, inasmuch as I am the apostle of the Gentiles, I magnify mine office: (Romans 11: 13)

Whereunto I am ordained a preacher, and an apostle, (I speak the truth in Christ, and lie not;) a teacher of the Gentiles in faith and verity. (1 Timothy 2: 7)

Whereunto I am appointed a preacher, and an apostle, and a teacher of the Gentiles. (2 Timothy 1: 11)

As an apostle, sent to the Gentiles, he was given revelations concerning the mystery. The Greek word *musterion* is translated mystery twenty-seven times in the New Testament, twenty of them in the epistles of Paul, three in Matthew, Mark and Luke, and four in Revelation.

The Mystery Hid in Scripture

Now to him that is of power to stablish you according to my gospel, and the preaching of Jesus Christ, according to the revelation of the mystery, which was kept secret since the world began, But now is made manifest, and by the scriptures of the prophets, according to the commandment of the everlasting God, made known to all nations for the obedience of faith: (Romans 16: 25-26)

Why did God have to hide something in Scripture? **But we speak the wisdom of God in a mystery, even the hidden wisdom, which God ordained before the world unto our glory: Which none of the princes of this world knew: for had they known it, they would not have crucified the Lord of glory.** (1 Corinthians 2: 7-9) God hid the fact that through His death he would destroy Satan, who had the power over death. (Hebrews 2: 14) Also the death of Jesus would be a sacrifice for the sins of the world. (Hebrews 9: 26)

These above facts were either not known, or not understood by the 12 apostles, but they were revealed unto the apostle Paul. If the 12 obtained any understanding of these facts, they would have gotten them from Paul; for when Jesus mentioned His death to the disciples they did not know what He was saying, as is seen in the following:

And he began to teach them, that the Son of man must suffer many things, and be rejected of the elders, and of the chief priests, and scribes, and be killed, and after three days rise again. And he spake that saying openly. And Peter took him, and began to rebuke him. But when he had turned about and looked on his disciples, he rebuked Peter, saying, Get thee behind me, Satan: for thou savourest not the things that be of God, but the things that be of men. (Mark 8: 31-33)

And as they came down from the mountain, he charged them that they should tell no man what things they had seen, till the Son of man were risen from the dead. And they kept that saying with themselves, questioning one with another what the rising from the dead should mean. (Mark 9: 9-10)
And they departed thence, and passed through Galilee; and he would not that any man should know it. For he taught his disciples, and said unto them, The Son of man is delivered into the hands of men, and they shall kill him; and after that he is killed, he shall rise the third day. But they understood not that saying, and were afraid to ask him. (Mark 9: 30-32)

Saying, Behold, we go up to Jerusalem; and the Son of man shall be delivered unto the chief priests, and unto the scribes; and they shall condemn him to death, and shall deliver him to the Gentiles: And they shall mock him, and shall scourge him, and shall spit upon him, and shall kill him: and the third day he shall rise again. (Mark 10: 33-34)

Why didn't the twelve understand? Why did they not believe the Lord? They did not believe because the Lord was not ready for them to believe. They did not see what Old

Testament Scripture reveals to us today because the meaning was hid from them at the point in time. **And they understood none of these things: and this saying was <u>hid from them</u>, neither knew they the things which were spoken.** (Luke 18: 34)

Today, we preached that Christ died for our sins, was buried and rose again and that our sins are blotted out the moment we trust the completed work of Christ. Peter and the others did not preach that. This is what they preached: **Then Peter said unto them, Repent, and be <u>baptized</u> every one of you in the name of Jesus Christ <u>for the remission of sins</u>, and ye shall receive the gift of the Holy Ghost.** (Acts 2: 38) There is not one word in the passage that talks about Christ's blood for remission of sins or for blotting out of sins. Why? It was a secret that would be revealed unto Paul, and Paul is not saved until Acts 9.

The Pauline Epistles emphasize atonement for sins through the blood of Christ. Look at it: **"Having predestinated us unto the adoption of children by Jesus Christ to himself, according to the good pleasure of his will, To the praise of the glory of his grace, wherein he hath made us accepted in the beloved. In whom we have <u>redemption through his blood, the forgiveness of sins</u>, according to the riches of his grace;"** (Ephesians 1: 5-7) The preaching of the cross is all Pauline.

The Mystery Hid In God

Unto me, who am less than the least of all saints, is this grace given, that I should preach among the Gentiles the <u>unsearchable</u> riches of Christ; And to make all men see what is the fellowship of the mystery, which from the

beginning of the world hath been hid in God, who created all things by Jesus Christ: (Ephesians 3: 8-9)

In Ephesians 3, we see that Paul was given:

1. A Gentile ministry (3: 1)
2. The Dispensation of Grace (3: 2)
3. The Mystery (3: 3)
4. The mission to proclaim to the Gentiles the grace ministry (3: 6-8)
5. The job of revealing what had been hid in God (3: 9)

Paul received the Mystery and passed it on to other apostles and prophets of the day. The Mystery is mentioned twelve times in the Prison Epistles:

The mystery of His will (Ephesians 1: 9)
The mystery (Ephesians (3: 3)
The mystery of Christ ((Ephesians 3: 4)
The fellowship of the mystery (Ephesians 3: 9)
A great mystery (Ephesians 5: 32)
Them mystery of the gospel (Ephesians 6: 19)
The mystery....hid from ages and generations (Colossians 1: 26)
The mystery among the Gentiles (Colossians 1: 27)
The mystery of God (Colossians 2: 2)
The mystery of Christ (Colossians 4: 3)
The mystery of the faith (1Timothy 3: 9)
The mystery of godliness (I timothy 3: 16)

If you study these passages of Scripture you should notice:

1. The church the Body of Christ comes to the forefront.

2. This formation of the Body in this new dispensation signifies completeness in Christ and fullness for the Gentiles.
3. The mystery came about after having a revelation from God. God chooses to whom He imparted that revelation.
4. Paul was a chosen apostle with a special ministry, communicating his revelations to a select group of people during a specific period of time.

The Mystery Concerning the Gentiles

Perhaps you are wondering, "What is the importance of this Mystery and it's implications for the Gentile? Are Gentiles treated any differently today than they were in A.D. 33 or B.C. 40?" Those are good questions and there are Scriptural answers.

We have already seen the Jews considered the Gentiles to be second class citizens, they were often referred to as "dogs." (Matthew 15: 26) God had chosen the Jews to be a peculiar treasure. Psalms 135: 4: **For the Lord hath chosen Jacob unto himself and Israel for his peculiar treasure**. In God's eyes, they had an advantage; that is why he gave them the law. Romans 3: 1-2: **What advantage then hath the Jew? or what profit is there of circumcision? Much every way: chiefly, because that unto them were committed the oracles of God.**

In Paul's early ministry, he acknowledged the gospel of Christ was to the Jew first. Romans 1: 16: **For I am not ashamed of the gospel of Christ: for it is the power of God unto salvation to every one that believeth; <u>to the Jew first</u>, and also to the Greek.**

Then Paul stood up, and beckoning with his hand said, Men of Israel, and ye that fear God, give audience. The God of this people of Israel chose our fathers, and exalted the people when they dwelt as strangers in the land of Egypt, and with an high arm brought he them out of it. ...Men and brethren, children of the stock of Abraham, and whosoever among you feareth God, to you is the word of this salvation sent. (Acts 13: 16-17; 26)

After having read the verse above, I see:

1. The Jew definitely had an advantage at one point in time.
2. The Jewish proselytes (Gentiles who had been circumcised) also had an advantage.
3. Salvation was sent to the Jew first, and those who feared God. (Gentiles)

Being a Gentile during Old Testament days and in Matthew – John, meant one was at a disadvantage. God gave the promises to the Jews. If a Gentile was to receive the promises, he would have to renounce his pagan ways and be circumcised. Even then, upon entering into the Synagogue, he was relegated a seating position behind those who's birthright was Jewish. The Gentile was alienated because of their birthright.

Wherefore remember, that ye being in time past Gentiles in the flesh, who are called Uncircumcision by that which is called the Circumcision in the flesh made by hands; That at that time ye were without Christ, being aliens from the commonwealth of Israel, and strangers from the covenants of promise, having no hope, and without God in the world: But now in Christ Jesus ye who some-

times were far off are made nigh by the blood of Christ. (Ephesians 2: 11-13)

To whom God would make known what is the riches of the glory of this mystery among the Gentiles; which is Christ in you, the hope of glory: (Colossians 1: 27) What is the riches of the glory of this mystery among Gentiles? Redemption! If a Gentile refused to fear God, do works of righteousness and become a circumcised proselyte, he had no hope and was without God. But the mystery concerning the Gentiles provided hope. When Israel became Loammi God revealed the mystery concerning the Gentiles. The Gentiles would become the chosen ones to spread the good news of Christ's death, burial and resurrection for the remission of sins.

And so, the Dispensation of the Grace of God is all about Gentiles being the favored of God. Israel had to be set aside before this dispensation could begin. With the diminishing of the roll of the Jew in spreading the gospel came the rising of the Gentile. Now that Israel has been set aside, temporarily, God could show grace to every Gentile, those who blessed Israel and those who did not.

FACT: In this dispensation, whether or not you bless Israel or curse Israel has no bearing upon your relationship with God. Genesis 12: 1-3 does not apply in this Age of Grace. It did at one point in time, but not today. Jewish people can be saved today, but they have to go against their religious leaders and believe Christ has come and that He alone can guarantee them an inheritance with God.

The foundation laid by Paul is the only acceptable way of salvation for the 21st Century. If you are basing your salvation on the foundation laid by Peter, you are in for a rude awakening. Peter is not the Rock upon which God will built His church in this dispensation. Christ is the Rock, whether in this dispensation, past dispensations or future ones.

And Jesus answered and said unto him, Blessed art thou, Simon Barjona: for flesh and blood hath not revealed it unto thee, but my Father which is in heaven. And I say also unto thee, That thou art Peter, and upon this rock I will build my church; and the gates of hell shall not prevail against it. (Matthew 16: 17-18)

There is a religious organization that has based their entire doctrinal position based upon Peter as the rock for the formation of the church. They believe that Peter was the first leader, and the church of the verse above is the Catholic church. They err! When shown 1 Peter 2: 4-8 they can never give a satisfactory answer. Look at the verses:

To whom coming, as unto <u>a living stone</u>, disallowed indeed of men, but <u>chosen of God</u>, and precious, Ye also, as lively stones, are built up a spiritual house, an holy priesthood, to offer up spiritual sacrifices, acceptable to God by <u>Jesus Christ</u>. Wherefore also it is contained in the scripture, Behold, <u>I lay in Sion a chief corner stone</u>, elect, precious: and he that believeth on him shall not be confounded. Ye also, as lively stones, are built up a spiritual house, an holy priesthood, to offer up spiritual sacrifices, acceptable to God by Jesus Christ. Unto you therefore which believe he is precious: but unto them which be disobedient, the stone which the builders disallowed, the same is made the head of the corner, And a stone of stumbling, and a rock of offence, even to them which stumble at the word, being disobedient: whereunto also they were appointed.

The chief cornerstone contained in the Scriptures was Jesus Christ, not Peter. Anyone who will believe on Christ, not Peter, shall not be confounded. Jesus is the rock on which the disobedient stumble. It is Jesus who is the rock of offense, not Peter.

If an entire religious order has been formed believing Peter is the founding father, the cornerstone, the rock, it cannot afford to change that position even though they know their founders made a mistake. Change is not going to happen for this religious persuasion. Why? Because they would have to admit that they were wrong. They would lose credibility and probably lose members. So what can they do? They will continue covering up and teaching a lie.

FACT: The foundation and cornerstone of the real church, whether it is the Church the Body of Christ or the physical church centered at Jerusalem, is Jesus Christ the Lord. **For other foundation can no man lay than that is laid, which is Jesus Christ.** (1 Corinthians 3: 11)

So then, what is Paul speaking of in 1 Corinthians 3: 10? **According to the grace of God which is given unto me, as a wise masterbuilder, <u>I have laid the foundation</u>, and another buildeth thereon. But let every man take heed how he buildeth thereupon.**

Paul says:

1. I have laid the foundation
   a. What is it?
   b. What is it for?
   c. To whom does it concern?
2. He cautions us to take heed on how he builds on that foundation.

Paul laid a foundation upon Christ, and that foundation is for the erection of a temple: **Know ye not that ye are the temple of God, and that the Spirit of God dwelleth in you?** (1 Corinthians 3: 16) That temple is you and me – the Church the Body of Christ. The foundation is not the gospel, for the gospel was laid out in Old Testament Scripture. So the foundation that Paul laid, with Jesus as the cornerstone of the temple, has something to do with the order of resurrection. Look at the following verses.

And he is the head of the body, the church: who is the beginning, the firstborn from the dead; that in all things he might have the preeminence. (Colossians 1: 18)

For as in Adam all die, even so in Christ shall all be made alive. But every man in his own order: Christ the firstfruits; afterward they that are Christ's at his coming. Then cometh the end, when he shall have delivered up the kingdom to God, even the Father; when he shall have put down all rule and all authority and power. For he must reign, till he hath put all enemies under his feet. (1 Corinthians 15: 22-25)

In the Corinthians passage, you will notice a definite order of resurrection: Christ and they that are Christ's at His coming. First, Christ comes in the air for the Body of Christ, and second, He comes back to earth for Israel. Then the end comes when he puts all enemies under his feet and all the lost will be resurrected to stand in judgment.

The fact that Jesus was coming again was no secret. Israel was waiting to be restored. But the fact that He would come for the Body of Christ before He came to restore Israel was a mystery, a secret hid in God. That is why Paul said: **Consider what I say; and the Lord give thee understanding in all**

things. Remember that Jesus Christ of the seed of David was raised from the dead according to my gospel: (2 Timothy 2: 7-8)

Peter spoke of Christ being resurrected to sit on David's earthly throne. Paul spoke of Christ being resurrected to sit at the right hand of the Father – a heavenly throne.

Did Peter and Paul preach the same gospel? No, they preached the same Christ, who is the chief cornerstone for both messages, but they preached differently concerning the resurrection.

Peter - Prophecy	Paul - Mystery
1) Gospel of the circumcision (Gal. 2: 7-9)	1) Gospel of the uncircumcision (Gal. 2: 7-9)
2) Sent to baptize (Mark 16: 14-18)	2) Not sent to baptize (1 Cor. 1: 17)
3) Baptism was for remission of sins (Acts 2: 38) The blotting out of sins is future (Acts 3: 1921)	3) Remission of sins and blotting out of sins is by the blood of Christ the moment one Believes. (Eph. 1: 7)
4) Ministry to Jews all over the world (Acts 1: 8)	4) Ministry to the Gentiles (Acts 9: 13-15; 26:15-17)
5) Message at Pentecost to Jews (Acts 2: 14-38)	5) Taught his believes to follow him as he followed Christ (1 Cor. 11: 1)
6) Pentecost, the beginning of restoration and Revival for Jews (Acts 2: 16-21)	6) Last days for Gentiles concerns apostasy, not revival (2 Tim. 3: 1-5; 4: 3-4)
7) Preached Christ resurrected to sit on David's throne on earth. (Acts 2: 25-31)	7) Preached Christ resurrected to sit at the right hand of God in heaven (Eph. 1: 20)
8) Earthly inheritance (Jer. 23: 5; Mat 5: 5)	8) Heavenly inheritance (Eph. 1: 3; Col. 3: 1-2)

Differences Between Prophecy and Mystery

Prophecy concerns Israel, the Old Testament prophets, the teaching of Jesus and Peter.

1. It concerns a literal kingdom on earth. (Jeremiah 23: 5)
2. It had been prophesied "since the world began." (Acts 3: 21)
3. Israel will be the dominant nation. (Isaiah 60: 12)

4. All people will follow Israel's lead for they know she is the chosen of God. (Zechariah 8: 23)
5. Christ returns for Israel to the earth. (Zechariah 14: 4)
6. Christ prepares twelve men to proclaim the start of restoration. (Acts 1: 6-8)

Mystery

1. This concerns a group of people with a heavenly inheritance (1 Cor. 12: 12, 27; Eph. 1: 3; 2: 6; 4: 12-16; Col. 3: 1-3)
2. It was chosen in Christ before the world began, but kept secret since the world began. (Eph. 1: 4; 3: 5-9; Rom. 16: 25-26)
3. There is one authoritarian figure and everyone is equal. (Rom. 10: 12; 11: 32; Eph. 2: 16-17)
4. Israel will not be the avenue of blessing because she is Loammi; Gentiles will be blessed because of Israel's fall. Rom. 11: 11-15; Acts 28: 27-28)
5. The mystery is about setting our affections on heaven and not earth. (Col. 3: 1-3; Eph. 1: 3)
6. The Lord prepares Paul to proclaim the mystery. (Eph. 3: 1-9; Col. 1: 24-27)

The saddest thing I have observed in the thirty plus years I have been in the ministry is the limited knowledge professing Christians have about the Word of God. Most do not realize what God has given them. They take grace for granted. They think the dispensation of grace has always been in existence. That is not so. Why do you think God chose the Body of Christ before the world began but chose to keep it a secret until He revealed it to Paul? Answer: to show His grace and so that Christ could be head of the body, which would be His fullness. **And hath put all things under his feet, and gave him to be the head over all things to the church,**

Which is his body, the fulness of him that filleth all in all.
(Ephesians 1: 22-23)

Once the body is complete Christ will be complete and the restoration of Israel can resume and be completed. Elijah will return and the full restoration will have begun. But until the rapture of the Church the Body of Christ, the restoration for Israel will not start.

Middle Wall

When did the Church the Body of Christ Begin?

That is a subject of much debate throughout Christendom. Many Bible believers do not think it is important, but I ask, what do you think?" If it is important, is there a passage of Scripture one must turn to for comfort and guidance? The answer is a resounding yes, and that verse is: **"Study to shew thyself approved unto God, a workman that needeth not to be ashamed, rightly dividing the word of truth."** 2 Timothy 2: 15.

This verse is the foundation for <u>right division</u>, words you will see often in print throughout this book; for it is the point of beginning for what I believe is the correct view in establishing the beginning of the body truth.

A high IQ is not a prerequisite to learning. I am not a Biblical scholar, and please do not get the impression in the following pages that I think all Biblical scholars are more interested in analogy rather than simple truth. I have read many books of some scholarly Biblical expositors and have been enlightened by some of their exposes. However, the man who has been most influential in my search for truth has been E. C. Moore.

E. C. Moore is not a college graduate, but he is a Biblical scholar. He has taught me how to allow the Word of God to speak for itself. He also taught me to read my Bible without preconceived ideas as to the meaning of a particular passage of Scripture. He said, "Read the Bible and allow the Holy Spirit to direct you." When reading this booklet, you should heed that advice also.

In your search for the beginning of the Church the Body of Christ it is very important that you rightly divide the Scriptures. In your search for truth, we will attempt to show you how you can draw your own conclusions on the subject at hand.

If you are a new Christian or if you have been a Christian without the benefit of having sat under a teacher of truth; you might not be aware that there are at least four views as to when the Church the Body of Christ began.

1. Covenant theology teaches the church of the Old Testament and the New Testament is one and the same.
2. Most fundamental evangelicals and many dispensationalists teach that the Body had its beginning on the day of Pentecost, as recorded in Acts chapter two.
3. There are other dispensationalists who recognize the distinctive ministry of Paul and take the mid-Acts (Acts 9-13) position for the starting point.

4. Then there are those dispensationalists that take the position that the Body began with the setting aside of Israel, which we find in Acts 28.

What I hope you will see from the four viewpoints listed above is that there is much emphasis placed by many Biblical scholars as to when and where the Church the Body of Christ began. Since that is the case, shouldn't it be a subject matter that is important enough to you to find who has taken the correct position, or more importantly to ask who has taken the correct Biblical position?

I want to be very clear. I have taken the position that the Church the Body of Christ began with the conversion of Paul in Acts chapter nine. I tell you this now so that you will not be wondering where I stand. You should know that the Acts 9 position I now take is different from what I grew up believing. My background is Southern Baptist, and for thirty-seven years I was, as most Baptists, of the Acts 2 persuasion.

I have written the following in a basic outline form. It is not intended to be a literary composition, it is meant to be informative. While I have a definite position, I hope the information given will allow you to make an informed decision based upon Scriptural evidence alone. My prayer is that you will allow the Holy Spirit to guide you through the following pages without any preconceived ideas from your denominational ties, if you have any.

Ephesians 2: 11-12: "11) **Wherefore remember, that ye being in <u>time past</u> Gentiles in the flesh, who are called Uncircumcision by that which is called the Circumcision in the flesh made by hands; 12) That <u>at that time</u> ye were without Christ, being aliens from the commonwealth**

of Israel, and strangers from the covenants of promise, having no hope, and without God in the world:"

Time Past: The time past of verse 11 is referring to a period of time prior to when Paul is writing this letter. It also is in reference to a period of time when the Jew considered the Gentiles to be an abomination to God. Whether or not that is true, it was the consensus thinking for that day and time.

In verse 12 Gentiles of time past were:

1) Uncircumcised,
2) Aliens from the commonwealth of Israel,
3) Strangers from the covenants of promise,
4) Having no hope, and
5) Without God in the world.

As you read any of the books I wrote, you will see me writing the following: "When you see a positive statement there is always a negative alternative." For instance, Romans 10:13 states: "For whosoever shall call upon the name of the Lord shall be saved." The negative alternative to that statement is: "For whosoever shall NOT call upon the name of the Lord shall NOT be saved."

In Ephesians we see a group of Gentiles who were definitely NOT saved. But apparently there were Gentiles:

1) Who had been circumcised,
2) Who were NOT aliens from the commonwealth of Israel,
3) Who were NOT strangers from the covenants of promise, or
4) Who did fear God.

It is a known fact that there were some Gentiles in Old Testament times that had favor with God. However, it is also a known fact that the Jew had more favor. When Abram was called by the Lord to leave his country and go to a place that the Lord would lead, he was a Gentile in the truest sense. He officially became a Jew when he was circumcised.

In Genesis 12: 1-3 we read:

1. **Now the Lord had said unto Abram, Get thee out of thy country, and from thy kindred, and from thy father's house, unto a land that I will shew thee:**
2. **And I will make of thee a great nation, and I will bless thee, and make thy name great; and thou shalt be a blessing:**
3. **And I will bless them that bless thee, and curse him that curseth thee: and in thee shall all families of the earth be blessed.**

A Gentile could receive the blessings of God if they would bless Abraham's seed. Using the positive and negative form of rationale, a Gentile would not receive the blessing of God if they did not bless Abraham's seed.

Fact:

1. At one time the Jew had the advantage over the Gentile: "**For I am not ashamed of the gospel of Christ: for it is the power of God unto salvation to every one that believeth; to the Jew first, and also to the Greek.**" Romans 1: 16.
2. There was some advantage in circumcision, or being a Jew. "**What advantage then hath the Jew? or what profit is there of circumcision? Much every way:**

chiefly, because that unto them were committed the oracles of God." Romans 3: 1-2. If, during that time, there was no advantage to circumcision, then why did Paul suggest that Timothy be circumcised?

Look at Acts 16: 1-4: "**Then came he to Derbe and Lystra: and, behold, a certain disciple was there, named Timotheus, the son of a certain woman, which was a Jewess, and believed; but his father was a Greek: Which was well reported of by the brethren that were at Lystra and Iconium. Him would Paul have to go forth with him; and took and circumcised him because of the Jews which were in those quarters: for they knew all that his father was a Greek. And as they went through the cities, they delivered them the decrees for to keep, that were ordained of the apostles and elders which were at Jerusalem.**"

3. Paul began his ministry teaching in the Jewish Synagogues. "**And he went into the synagogue, and spake boldly for the space of three months, disputing and persuading the things concerning the kingdom of God. But when divers were hardened, and believed not, but spake evil of that way before the multitude, he departed from them, and separated the disciples, disputing daily in the school of one Tyrannus. And this continued by the space of two years; so that all they which dwelt in Asia heard the word of the Lord Jesus, both Jews and Greeks.**" Acts 19: 8-10.

After some of the Jews of Ephesians disputed (argued) with him about what he taught, he left the Synagogue and began preaching in the home of a Gentile. Then he catches some flak from idol worshipping Gentiles about the teaching, known as "that way." If you will look at Acts 19: 23, you will see "that way" mentioned again. **"And the same time there arose no small stir about that way."**

> a.) In Ephesus, there were idol-worshipping Gentiles of the goddess Diana. **"For a certain man named Demetrius, a silversmith, which made silver shrines for Diana, brought no small gain unto the craftsmen;"**
> b.) Many of them were silversmiths who made idols of the goddess Diana for sale.
> c.) The sale of those idols was profitable and when Paul teaches they have no need for idols, it cuts into their profit. Paul is definitely hurting their business. **"Whom he called together with the workmen of like occupation, and said, Sirs, ye know that by this craft we have our wealth."**
> d.) The silversmiths realized that if they did not get rid of Paul their businesses might fold. **"Moreover ye see and hear, that not alone at Ephesus, but almost throughout all Asia, this Paul hath persuaded and turned away much people, saying that they be no gods, which are made with hands: So that not only this our craft is in danger to be set at nought; but also that the temple of the great goddess Diana should be despised, and her magnificence should be destroyed, whom all Asia and the world worshippeth."** Acts 19: 26-27.

So it is evident there are a group of Ephesian Gentiles who did not believe in the God of Abraham, Isaac and Jacob.

They also did not like the way that Paul taught concerning the Lord Jesus Christ. Why? They were idol worshippers.

Remember Genesis 12: 1-3:

> 1 **Now the Lord had said unto Abram, Get thee out of thy country, and from thy kindred, and from thy father's house, unto a land that I will shew thee:**
> 2. **And I will make of thee a great nation, and I will bless thee, and make thy name great; and thou shalt be a blessing:**
> 3. **And I will bless them that bless thee, and curse him that curseth thee: and in thee shall all families of the earth be blessed.**

With that in mind, let us look at what we have in Ephesus in Acts 19 and 20.

1. There were a group of Ephesian Gentiles meeting in the synagogue who were blessing Israel and therefore partakers of the covenants of promise.
2. There were a group of Ephesian Gentiles who were idol worshippers and they did not like Israel and therefore they were not partakers of the covenants of promise, they were aliens from the commonwealth of Israel and without the true and living God.
3. Careful study of Romans, 1st and 2nd Corinthians and Galatians will reveal that the majority of these people were Gentiles that were partakers of the covenants of promise, and they were also members of the Church the Body of Christ, the foundation laid by Paul. Look at 1 Corinthians 3: 10-17:
   > **10 According to the grace of God which is given unto me, as a wise masterbuilder, I**

have laid the foundation, and another buildeth thereon. But let every man take heed how he buildeth thereupon.

11 For other foundation can no man lay than that is laid, which is Jesus Christ.

12 Now if any man build upon this foundation gold, silver, precious stones, wood, hay, stubble;

13 Every man's work shall be made manifest: for the day shall declare it, because it shall be revealed by fire; and the fire shall try every man's work of what sort it is.

14 If any man's work abide which he hath built thereupon, he shall receive a reward.

15 If any man's work shall be burned, he shall suffer loss: but he himself shall be saved; yet so as by fire.

16 Know ye not that ye are the temple of God, and that the Spirit of God dwelleth in you?

17 If any man defile the temple of God, him shall God destroy; for the temple of God is holy, which temple ye are.

a) Paul laid the foundation of the temple (which is you and me), the Church the Body of Christ.

b) It is NOT the laying of the foundation of the gospel, as some believe, for the gospel was laid out (though hidden) in the Old Testament Scriptures.

1 Corinthians 15: 1-4:

1. Moreover, brethren, I declare unto you the gospel which I preached unto

you, which also ye have received, and wherein ye stand;
2. By which also ye are saved, if ye keep in memory what I preached unto you, unless ye have believed in vain.
3. For I delivered unto you first of all that which I also received, how that Christ died for our sins <u>according to the scriptures</u>;
4. And that he was buried, and that he rose again the third day <u>according to the scriptures:</u>

I have underlined the words "according to the Scriptures." This can only mean Old Testament Scripture.

c) The foundation that Paul laid is for the Church the Body of Christ – the temple of God, or if you will, the dwelling-place of God in this present dispensation. 1 Corinthians 3: 10-17, listed above, matches perfectly with Ephesians 2: 19-20: **"Now therefore ye are no more strangers and foreigners, but fellowcitizens with the saints, and of the household of God; And are built upon the foundation of the apostles and prophets, Jesus Christ himself being the chief corner stone;"** as well as with 2 Timothy 2: 19-20: **"Nevertheless the foundation of God standeth sure, having this seal, The Lord knoweth them that are his. And, Let every one that nameth the name of Christ depart from iniquity. But in a great house there are not only vessels of gold and of silver, but also of wood and of earth; and some** to honour, and some to dishonour." The foundation that Paul laid is Jesus Christ, and then Church the Body of Christ is built on the same foundation the Jews have – Jesus Christ.

d) Anyone who does not believe the gospel of Christ that Paul preaches is not a member of the Body of Christ. 2 Corinthians 4: 3-4: **"But if our gospel be hid, it is hid to them that are lost: In whom the god of this world hath blinded the minds of them which believe not, lest the light of the glorious gospel of Christ, who is the image of God, should shine unto them."**

e) The foundation of the Church the Body of Christ, which Paul preached, has to do with the order of resurrection. **"And he is the head of the body, the church: who is the beginning, the firstborn from the dead; that in all [things] he might have the preeminence."**

f) And Paul's preaching of resurrection is different from that which Peter preached. **"Consider what I say; and the Lord give thee understanding in all things. Remember that Jesus Christ of the seed of David was raised from the dead according to my gospel:"** Paul preached being resurrection to be seated at the right hand of God – in Heaven. Peter preached being resurrection to live with Jesus, the King, on earth.

When speaking concerning the Jews, Paul, in his letter to the Romans said: **"I say then, Have they stumbled that they should fall? God forbid: but rather through their** fall salvation is come unto the Gentiles, for to provoke them to jealousy." Romans 11: 11.

We see that God, in His wisdom, raised up Paul to be an apostle to the Gentiles, knowing that eventually it would provoke the Jews to jealousy and then perhaps they would turn back to God. This was prophesied to happen, even though God always kept Jacob as the apple of His eye, as is found in Deuteronomy 32: 9-10: **"For the Lord's portion is his people; Jacob is the lot of his inheritance. He found him in a desert land, and in the waste howling wilderness; he led him about, he instructed him, he kept him as the apple of his eye."** He knew they would turn from Him, as we see prophesied in Deuteronomy 32: 15-21:

> 15 But Jeshurun waxed fat, and kicked: thou art waxen fat, thou art grown thick, thou art covered with fatness; then he forsook God which made him, and lightly esteemed the Rock of his salvation.
> 16 They provoked him to jealousy with strange gods, with abominations provoked they him to anger.
> 17 They sacrificed unto devils, not to God; to gods whom they knew not, to new gods that came newly up, whom your fathers feared not.
> 18 Of the Rock that begat thee thou art unmindful, and hast forgotten God that formed thee.
> 19 And when the Lord saw it, he abhorred them, because of the provoking of his sons, and of his daughters.
> 20 And he said, I will hide my face from them, I will see what their end shall be: for they are a very froward generation, children in whom is no faith.
> 21 They have moved me to jealousy with that which is not God; they have provoked me to anger with their vanities: and I will move them to jealousy

with those which are not a people; I will provoke them to anger with a foolish nation.

It was God's intention to one day make Gentiles a special people even before he called Abram out of Haran. "**Blessed be the God and Father of our Lord Jesus Christ, who hath blessed us with all spiritual blessings in heavenly places in Christ: According as he hath <u>chosen us in him before the foundation of the world</u>, that we should be holy and without blame before him in love: Having predestinated us unto the adoption of children by Jesus Christ to himself, according to the good pleasure of his will, To the praise of the glory of his grace, wherein he hath made us accepted in the beloved.**" Ephesians 1: 3-6.

Did this mean that God intended Israel to be a second class people? God forbid! For Paul also was informed by the Lord that even though Israel would fall, their fullness would be complete in due time. "**Now if the fall of them be the riches of the world, and the diminishing of them the riches of the Gentiles; how much more their fulness?**" Romans 11: 11.

It must be noted, according to the prophecy of Deuteronomy 32, the Lord would hide His face from Israel for a period of time. This time period would come to be known as the Dispensation of Grace, the period of time in which we now live, the 21st Century. Israel is Lo-ammi (not my people.) She has gone a whoring from God, and God has been provoked to anger and turned His back on her. And He will not bring her back into favor until the time of the fullness of the Gentiles.

In real time, today, Israel is cut off from the blessings of God Almighty. In the eleventh chapter of Romans, the olive tree represents Israel's privileges and unbelieving Israel is that broken branch. "**For if the firstfruit be holy, the lump is** also holy: and if the root be holy, so are the branches. And if some of the branches be broken off, and thou, being a wild olive tree, wert graffed in among them, and with them partakest of the root and fatness of the olive tree;" Romans 11: 16-17.

The Gentiles are being grafted into that tree and receive their blessings because of Israel's fall, but Israel will be rewarded in the end. Romans 11: 25-27: **"For I would not, brethren, that ye should be ignorant of this mystery, lest ye should be wise in your own conceits; that blindness in part is happened to Israel, until the fulness of the Gentiles be come in And so all Israel shall be saved: as it is written, There shall come out of Sion the Deliverer, and shall turn away ungodliness from Jacob: For this is my covenant unto them, when I shall take away their sins."**

In Romans 15: 25-27 we see Paul taking up a collection for the Jewish saints who are still alive and living in Jerusalem. **"But now I go unto Jerusalem to minister unto the saints. For it hath pleased them of Macedonia and Achaia to make a certain contribution for the poor saints which are at Jerusalem. It hath pleased them verily; and their debtors they are. For if the Gentiles have been made partakers of their spiritual things, their duty is also to minister unto them in carnal things."**

A Gentile who feared God could be grafted into the tree also. Acts 13: 16: **"Then Paul stood up, and beckoning with his hand said, Men of Israel, and ye that fear God, give audience.** Acts 13: 26: **"Men and brethren, children of the stock of Abraham, and whosoever among you feareth God, to you is the word of this salvation sent."**

During the Acts period, we find that the hope of Israel was extended to the Gentiles. But we also see that Paul was imprisoned for the hope of Israel. "**For this cause therefore have I called for you, to see you, and to speak with you: because that for the hope of Israel I am bound with this chain.**" Acts 28:20

In Acts 28: 24-28, we see that Israel became Lo-Ammi. "**And some believed the things which were spoken, and some believed not. And when they agreed not among themselves, they departed, after that Paul had spoken one word, Well spake the Holy Ghost by Esaias the prophet unto our fathers, Saying, Go unto this people, and say, Hearing ye shall hear, and shall not understand; and seeing ye shall see, and not perceive: For the heart of this people is waxed gross, and their ears are dull of hearing, and their eyes have they closed; lest they should see with their eyes, and hear with their ears, and understand with their heart, and should be converted, and I should heal them.**"

Israel's hope had to do with a city in the heavens, not far above all, heavens, for that is reserved for the Body of Christ.

When the setting aside of Israel happens, a new hope was extended to the Gentiles. Ephesians 3: 1-6:

1. **For this cause I Paul, the prisoner of Jesus Christ for you Gentiles,**
2. **If ye have heard of the dispensation of the grace of God which is given me to you-ward:**
3. **How that by revelation he made known unto me the mystery; (as I wrote afore in few words,**
4. **Whereby, when ye read, ye may understand my knowledge in the mystery of Christ)**

5. Which in other ages was not made known unto the sons of men, as it is now revealed unto his holy apostles and prophets by the Spirit;
6. That the Gentiles should be fellowheirs, and of the same body, and partakers of his promise in Christ by the gospel:

This new hope for Gentiles means that the religious privileges for Israel have been set aside – temporarily. It also means that God can fulfil His commitment to the Gentiles which he had planned before the foundation of the world. **"According as he hath chosen us in him before the foundation of the world, that we should be holy and without blame before him in love:"**

Ephesians 2: 13-18:

13 But now in Christ Jesus ye who sometimes were far off are made nigh by the blood of Christ.
14 For he is our peace, who hath made both one, and hath broken down the middle wall of partition between us;
15 Having abolished in his flesh the enmity, even the law of commandments contained in ordinances; for to make in himself of twain one new man, so making peace;
16 And that he might reconcile both unto God in one body by the cross, having slain the enmity thereby:
17 And came and preached peace to you which were afar off, and to them that were nigh.
18 For through him we both have access by one Spirit unto the Father.

In verse 13, the "now in Christ Jesus" is set in contrast to "time past" as mentioned in the verses 11 & 12. The people to whom verse 13 is addressed used to have no hope, but now have a hope. Those who were without God now have God. Those who were aliens from the commonwealth of Israel and strangers from the covenants of promise are now nigh by the blood of Christ. Why? They have been reconciled (v.16) by the cross.

Notice it does not say they were reconciled at the cross. For the believer who studies the Word of truth rightly divided, will see that the Jew was still the means of hope up to and until the time of their being set aside.

Those Who First Trusted vs. Those Who Trusted At a Later Date

Look at the following verses. Ephesians 1: 9-13:

> **9 Having made known unto us the mystery of his will, according to his good pleasure which he hath purposed in himself:**
> **10 That in the dispensation of the fulness of times he might gather together in one all things in Christ, both which are in heaven, and which are on earth; [even] in him:**
> **11 In whom also we have obtained an inheritance, being predestinated according to the purpose of him who worketh all things after the counsel of his own will:**
> **12 That we should be to the praise of his glory, who first trusted in Christ.**
> **13 In whom ye also trusted, after that ye heard the word of truth, the gospel of your salvation: in**

whom also after that ye believed, ye were sealed with that holy Spirit of promise,

You need to take the time to read Ephesians 1 & 2. When you do, I want you to look at some key words in the passages of these two chapter, they are: us, we and ye. They will play an important role in helping you understand the truth of the Word rightly divided.

1. In verse 12 we are apprised of a group of believers who first trusted in Christ.
2. In verse 13 we see another group of believers who also trusted. Paul refers to those as "ye".
3. Both groups of people are members of the Body of Christ.

Ephesians 2: 1-7:

1 And you hath he quickened, who were dead in trespasses and sins;
2 Wherein in time past ye walked according to the course of this world, according to the prince of the power of the air, the spirit that now worketh in the children of disobedience:
3 Among whom also we all had our conversation in times past in the lusts of our flesh, fulfilling the desires of the flesh and of the mind; and were by nature the children of wrath, even as others.
4 But God, who is rich in mercy, for his great love wherewith he loved us,
5 Even when we were dead in sins, hath quickened us together with Christ, (by grace ye are saved;)
6 And hath raised us up together, and made us sit together in heavenly places in Christ Jesus:

> 7 That in the ages to come he might shew the exceeding riches of his grace in his kindness toward us through Christ Jesus.

After having read the verses above, you should have noticed several things in the passages. The people listed as "ye" were dead in trespasses and sin and walked according to the world and Satan. You will also notice in verse 5 that they were saved by grace.

You should have also seen that the first group of believers had problems with the flesh and were children of wrath the same as the "ye" group.

Both groups are loved by God and have been quickened together with Christ and raised up together to sit in heavenly places, thereby indicating that both groups were a part of the Body of Christ.

Ephesians 2: 8-16:

> 8 For by grace are ye saved through faith; and that not of yourselves: it is the gift of God:
> 9 Not of works, lest any man should boast.
> 10 For we are his workmanship, created in Christ Jesus unto good works, which God hath before ordained that we should walk in them.
> 11 Wherefore remember, that ye being in time past Gentiles in the flesh, who are called Uncircumcision by that which is called the Circumcision in the flesh made by hands;
> 12 That at that time ye were without Christ, being aliens from the commonwealth of Israel, and strangers from the covenants of promise, having no hope, and without God in the world:

13 But now in Christ Jesus ye who sometimes were far off are made nigh by the blood of Christ.
14 For he is our peace, who hath made both one, and hath broken down the middle wall of partition between us;
15 Having abolished in his flesh the enmity, even the law of commandments contained in ordinances; for to make in himself of twain one new man, so making peace;
16 And that he might reconcile both unto God in one body by the cross, having slain the enmity thereby:

These two groups of Gentiles had some issues among themselves, and Ephesians 2: 14 says there had been a middle wall of partition between them that was now broken down. Then in verse 15 we find this wall had been abolished by Jesus Christ. The verse explains it was the law of commandments contained in ordinances that had been abolished and had been the problem between the two groups of Gentiles.

In Ephesian 2: 16 he notes that the reconciliation of the two groups was a result of the death of Jesus Christ. Notice the passage says "by the cross." It does not say the reconciliation occurred at the cross. I know that to be true because of what Peter said in Acts10: 28: "**And he said unto them, Ye know how that it is an unlawful thing for a man that is a Jew to keep company, or come unto one of another nation; but God hath shewed me that I should not call any man common or unclean**." Peter knew that the law of commandments contained in ordinances was still very much in operation for the Jew.

In Ephesians 2: 15 we see that with the abolishing of the enmity, the law, these two groups could be made one –

become one new man. This new man had not been in existence before. The body of Christ was fragmented because those who first believe had an obligation to continue to observe certain ordinances. Look at the following passages.

James is speaking in Acts 15: 19-21: **"Wherefore my sentence is, that we trouble not them, which from among the Gentiles are turned to God: But that we write unto them, that they abstain from pollutions of idols, and from fornication, and from things strangled, and from blood. For Moses of old time hath in every city them that preach him, being read in the synagogues every sabbath day."** He is telling the Jews that Gentiles who had turned to God should not be troubled, but they should be asked to refrain from things strangled and from blood.

Acts 16: 1-3: **"Then came he to Derbe and Lystra: and, behold, a certain disciple was there, named Timotheus, the son of a certain woman, which was a Jewess, and believed; but his father was a Greek: Which was well reported of by the brethren that were at Lystra and Iconium. Him would Paul have to go forth with him; and took and circumcised him because of the Jews which were in those quarters: for they knew all that his father was a Greek."** Because Timothy was part Jew, Paul thought it best that he be circumcised, thereby observing the ordinance of circumcision.

Galatians 2: 1-3: **"Then fourteen years after I went up again to Jerusalem with Barnabas, and took Titus with me also. And I went up by revelation, and communicated unto them that gospel which I preach among the Gentiles, but privately to them which were of reputation, lest by any means I should run, or had run, in vain. And I went up by revelation, and communicated unto them that**

gospel which I preach among the Gentiles, but privately to them which were of reputation, lest by any means I should run, or had run, in vain." Paul did not consider having Titus circumcised since he was a Greek (Gentile).

When Paul began his ministry, he was to be all things to all people. He did not want to offend the Jew, nor did he want to burden the Gentile with Jewish commandments. His early ministry was filled with instances where the Jewish hierarchy was always questioning his authority and the validity of his message. By the time he wrote the Ephesian letter God had revealed unto him it was time to quit appeasing the Jew, for they had been set aside (become Lo-Ammi).

As we have mentioned before, the letters Paul wrote to the Romans, Corinthians and Galatians were filled with things they were to do, in the hopes that by doing them they might not offend the Jew and thereby help them see the truth.

The Gentiles who first believed and those who believed later were all part of the Body of Christ.

1 Corinthians 12: 12-14: "**For as the body is one, and hath many members, and all the members of that one body, being many, are one body: so also is Christ. For by one Spirit are we all baptized into one body, whether we be Jews or Gentiles, whether we be bond or free; and have been all made to drink into one Spirit. For the body is not one member, but many.**"

1 Corinthians 12: 27-31: "**Now ye are the body of Christ, and members in particular. And God hath set some in the church, first apostles, secondarily prophets, thirdly teachers, after that miracles, then gifts of healings, helps, governments, diversities of tongues. Are all apostles?**

are all prophets? are all teachers? are all workers of miracles? Have all the gifts of healing? do all speak with tongues? do all interpret? But covet earnestly the best gifts: and yet shew I unto you a more excellent way."

You will notice that in Paul's early ministry there were categories of importance. There were those who had certain gifts. But it was evident that all the people did not have all of the gifts. It should also be note that when Paul lists the gifts in Ephesians, he eliminates quite a few of those listed in 1 Corinthians 12.

Ephesians 4: 8: "**Wherefore he saith, When he ascended up on high, he led captivity captive, and gave gifts unto men.**"

Ephesians 4: 11: "**And he gave some, apostles; and some, prophets; and some, evangelists; and some, pastors and teachers;**"

When the two groups of Gentiles become the "one new man," one does not think of himself as getting better or worse but the same.

Ephesians 3: 1-3, 6:
"**For this cause I Paul, the prisoner of Jesus Christ for you Gentiles, If ye have heard of the dispensation of the grace of God which is given me to you-ward: How that by revelation he made known unto me the mystery; (as I wrote afore in few words,... That the Gentiles should be fellowheirs, and of the same body, and partakers of his promise in Christ by the gospel:**"

The Body of Christ is a unified body of believers and one of its goals is to become a perfect man.

Ephesians 4: 11-16:

> 11 And he gave some, apostles; and some, prophets; and some, evangelists; and some, pastors and teachers;
> 12 For the perfecting of the saints, for the work of the ministry, for the edifying of the body of Christ:
> 13 Till we all come in the unity of the faith, and of the knowledge of the Son of God, unto <u>a perfect man</u>, unto the measure of the stature of the fulness of Christ:
> 14 That we henceforth be no more children, tossed to and fro, and carried about with every wind of doctrine, by the sleight of men, and cunning craftiness, whereby they lie in wait to deceive;
> 15 But speaking the truth in love, may grow up into him in all things, which is the head, even Christ:
> 16 From whom the whole body fitly joined together and compacted by that which every joint supplieth, according to the effectual working in the measure of every part, maketh increase of the body unto the edifying of itself in love.

This perfect man in Ephesians 4: 13 is the same one new man of Ephesians 2: 15: "**Having abolished in his flesh the enmity, even the law of commandments contained in ordinances; for to make in himself of twain <u>one new man</u>, so making peace;**"

That man is made perfect and new by the breaking down of the middle wall of partition, and both of them becoming united in one body in Christ Jesus; and none being better than the other, none having the restrictions of ordinances being imposed on them.

The reason it is necessary to become this new and perfect man is stated in Ephesians 4: 14: **"That we henceforth be no more children, tossed to and fro, and carried about with every wind of doctrine, ..."**

If you are a Christian, you have probably been more confused about ordinances than any other topic. Should we do this or shouldn't we? How do we do it? When do we practice it? In what name are we doing it? This issues that arise over baptism and communion have been the reason many in Christendom have left the church, and that is so sad. Why? These ordinances were abolished by the cross.

The second chapter of Colossians gives a pretty good picture of the condition of the new and perfect man. Colossians 2: 6-23:

> **6 As ye have therefore received Christ Jesus the Lord, so walk ye in him:**
> **7 Rooted and built up in him, and stablished in the faith, as ye have been taught, abounding therein with thanksgiving.**
> **8 Beware lest any man spoil you through philosophy and vain deceit, after the tradition of men, after the rudiments of the world, and not after Christ.**
> **9 For in him dwelleth all the fulness of the Godhead bodily.**
> **10 And ye are complete in him, which is the head of all principality and power:**
> **11 In whom also ye are circumcised with the circumcision made without hands, in putting off the body of the sins of the flesh by the circumcision of Christ:**
> **12 Buried with him in baptism, wherein also ye are risen with him through the faith of the operation of God, who hath raised him from the dead.**

13 And you, being dead in your sins and the uncircumcision of your flesh, hath he quickened together with him, having forgiven you all trespasses;

14 Blotting out the handwriting of ordinances that was against us, which was contrary to us, and took it out of the way, nailing it to his cross;

15 And having spoiled principalities and powers, he made a shew of them openly, triumphing over them in it.

16 Let no man therefore judge you in meat, or in drink, or in respect of an holyday, or of the new moon, or of the sabbath days:

17 Which are a shadow of things to come; but the body is of Christ.

18 Let no man beguile you of your reward in a voluntary humility and worshipping of angels, intruding into those things which he hath not seen, vainly puffed up by his fleshly mind,

19 And not holding the Head, from which all the body by joints and bands having nourishment ministered, and knit together, increaseth with the increase of God.

20 Wherefore if ye be dead with Christ from the rudiments of the world, why, as though living in the world, are ye subject to ordinances,

21 (Touch not; taste not; handle not;

22 Which all are to perish with the using;) after the commandments and doctrines of men?

23 Which things have indeed a shew of wisdom in will worship, and humility, and neglecting of the body; not in any honour to the satisfying of the flesh.

What do these verses say about those of us who are members of the Body of Christ?

v. 10	We are complete in Christ
v. 11	We are circumcised with Christ
v. 12	We are buried with Christ in Baptism
v. 12	We are dead with Christ
v. 13	We are quickened together with Christ
v. 13	Christ has forgiven ALL (not just a few) of my trespasses
v. 14	Christ blotted out the ordinances that were against us, nailing it to His cross
v. 15	Christ spoiled Satan and his follower's hope when he was resurrected
v. 16	Christ warns of those who would impose restriction of the law
v. 18	Christ said do not listen to those who would have you get involved in angel worship
vs. 19-23	Since you are dead with Christ, buried with Christ and risen with Christ, you are not to be concerned with the perishable things of this world. To do those things only proves you have a will power, something in which you can boast. Doing them does not bring honor to your Lord.

Religious organizations want their members to be obedient to the doctrine of the physical church. They are constantly bombarding members with "you must be baptized, you must go to confession, you cannot eat certain foods, and you must not associate with a certain crowd." While some of these might be good for your physical bodies, they do nothing for improving the spirit. Ritualistic tools used in worship are not of God for the Dispensation of Grace, the period of time in which we now live.

The Scripture says that when Christ died, ordinances died. Who are you going to believe, the Bible or a church ordinance? Christ fulfilled the Law. To continue observing ordinance is to rebel against the Word of God. We are to put away earthly things and think about heavenly things.

Colossians 3: 1-4:

1 If ye then be risen with Christ, seek those things which are above, where Christ sitteth on the right hand of God.
2 Set your affection on things above, not on things on the earth.
3 For ye are dead, and your life is hid with Christ in God.
4 When Christ, who is our life, shall appear, then shall ye also appear with him in glory.

And why do you suppose we are to think about heavenly things? Because we are already there, spiritually. Ephesians 2: 6: **And hath raised us up together, and made us sit together in heavenly places in Christ Jesus:**

Conclusion:

The Church the Body of Christ had to have begun with Paul. Why? Israel failed in her responsibility to be the spokesperson for the Lord Jesus Christ, so God raised up Paul to be the apostle to the Gentiles. Romans 11: 13: "**For I speak to you Gentiles, inasmuch as I am the apostle of the Gentiles, I magnify mine office:**" So the Body of Christ could not have begun before Acts 9. Paul was called to present the gospel to the uncircumcised Gentile and Peter and the twelve were called to present the gospel to the circumcised Jews.

Galatians 2: 7-9:

> 7 But contrariwise, when they saw that the gospel of the uncircumcision was committed unto me, as the gospel of the circumcision was unto Peter;
> 8 For he that wrought effectually in Peter to the apostleship of the circumcision, the same was mighty in me toward the Gentiles:)
> 9 And when James, Cephas, and John, who seemed to be pillars, perceived the grace that was given unto me, they gave to me and Barnabas the right hands of fellowship; that we should go unto the heathen, and they unto the circumcision.

At the beginning of this book, we said:

1. Covenant theology teaches the church of the Old Testament and the New Testament is one and the same.
2. Most fundamental evangelicals and many dispensationalists teach that the Body had its beginning on the day of Pentecost, as recorded in Acts chapter two.
3. There are other dispensationalists who recognize the distinctive ministry of Paul and take the mid-Acts (Acts 9-13) position for the starting point.
4. Then there are those dispensationalists that take the position that the Body began with the setting aside of Israel, which we find in Acts 28.

If you have read the information we have presented, you should have seen that people who take position number one are way off base.

Those who take position number two, do so because it is here that we see the outpouring of the Holy Spirit as evidence of something new. However, the disciples were not looking for the creation of a new body of believers, they were looking for Christ to restore the promised early kingdom.

Those who take position number four say the body must have begun when Israel was declared Lo-Ammi. If that were the case, why do we see body truth in the early writings of Paul? There was a change in Acts 28, but it was not concerning the formation of the Body of Christ, but rather to the finalization of dispensational change.

Perhaps you are wondering why religious scholars differ so much on the subject. I do not know of a certainty, but I suspect it has something to do with their lack of regard to the distinctive ministry of Paul.

Let me show you how I divide the Book of Acts.

Chapters Preached	City	Figure	People	Gospel	Paul
1-12	Jerusalem	Peter	Jews	Gospel of God	
13-19	Antioch	Paul & Others	Jews & Gentiles	Gospel of Christ	
17-28	Rome	Paul	Gentiles	Gospel of the Grace of God	

Do not get the impression that I believe Paul preached three separate Gospels, he did not. But for the purposes of teaching, I want to show you how his teaching progressed according to the revelations (plural) he received from God.

2 Corinthians 12: 1: **"It is not expedient for me doubtless to glory. I will come to visions and revelations of the Lord."**

2 Corinthians 12: 7: **"And lest I should be exalted above measure through the abundance of the revelations, there was given to me a thorn in the flesh, the messenger of Satan to buffet me, lest I should be exalted above measure."**

In acts 9, Paul is on his way to Damascus to capture followers of Jesus. **"And Saul, yet breathing out threatenings and slaughter against the disciples of the Lord, went unto the high priest, And desired of him letters to Damascus to the synagogues, that if he found any of this way, whether they were men or women, he might bring them bound unto Jerusalem."** Acts 9: 1-2.

But instead of capturing followers of Jesus he becomes a follower of Jesus.

> 12 And I thank Christ Jesus our Lord, who hath enabled me, for that he counted me faithful, putting me into the ministry;
> 13 Who was before a blasphemer, and a persecutor, and injurious: but I obtained mercy, because I did it ignorantly in unbelief.
> 14 And the grace of our Lord was exceeding abundant with faith and love which is in Christ Jesus.
> 15 This is a faithful saying, and worthy of all acceptation, that Christ Jesus came into the world to save sinners; of whom I am chief.
> 16 Howbeit for this cause I obtained mercy, that in me first Jesus Christ might shew forth all longsuffering, <u>for a pattern</u> to them which should hereafter believe on him to life everlasting.

So, Saul is saved and God says that he is a pattern, someone to be followed, to Gentile believers.

In early Acts Saul/Paul preaches what we have labeled the Gospel of God. **"And straightway he preached Christ in the synagogues, that he is the Son of God."** The Gospel of God is simply that Jesus was the Son of God. Saul had authority from the Jewish High Priest to bring people who confessed that Jesus was the Son of God back to Jerusalem for trail of heresy.

So Saul began to teach exactly what the disciples were teaching about Jesus. First Peter, **"He saith unto them, But whom say ye that I am? And Simon Peter answered and said, Thou art the Christ, the Son of the living God."** Matthew 16: 15-16.

And then Philip, Acts 8: 5: **"Then Philip went down to the city of Samaria, and preached Christ unto them."**

Acts 8: 29-37:

> 29 **Then the Spirit said unto Philip, Go near, and join thyself to this chariot.**
> 30 **And Philip ran thither to him, and heard him read the prophet Esaias, and said, Understandest thou what thou readest?**
> 31 **And he said, How can I, except some man should guide me? And he desired Philip that he would come up and sit with him.**
> 32 **The place of the scripture which he read was this, He was led as a sheep to the slaughter; and like a lamb dumb before his shearer, so opened he not his mouth:**
> 33 **In his humiliation his judgment was taken away: and who shall declare his generation? for his life is taken from the earth.**

> 34 And the eunuch answered Philip, and said, I pray thee, of whom speaketh the prophet this? of himself, or of some other man?
> 35 Then Philip opened his mouth, and began at the same scripture, and preached unto him Jesus.
> 36 And as they went on their way, they came unto a certain water: and the eunuch said, See, here is water; what doth hinder me to be baptized?
> 37 And Philip said, If thou believest with all thine heart, thou mayest. And he answered and said, I believe that <u>Jesus Christ is the Son of God</u>.

The passage the eunuch was reading was Isaiah 53: 7: "**He was oppressed, and he was afflicted, yet he opened not his mouth: he is brought as a lamb to the slaughter, and as a sheep before her shearers is dumb, so he openeth not his mouth.**" So, the Old Testament predicted that Jesus would come and die for the sins of many.

So Saul begins to teach to the ones he was sent to destroy. "**But they had heard only, That he which persecuted us in times past now preacheth the faith which once he destroyed.**" Acts 1: 23.

Peter, Philip and Paul are proving that Jesus is the Christ of prophecy. "**But Saul increased the more in strength, and confounded the Jews which dwelt at Damascus, proving that this is very Christ.**"

Paul goes into the Arabian desert. Galatians 1: 15-18:

> 15 But when it pleased God, who separated me from my mother's womb, and called me by his grace,

> 16 To reveal his Son in me, that I might preach him among the heathen; immediately I conferred not with flesh and blood:
> 17 Neither went I up to Jerusalem to them which were apostles before me; but I went into Arabia, and returned again unto Damascus.
> 18 Then after three years I went up to Jerusalem to see Peter, and abode with him fifteen days.

If we are following Paul's teaching in Acts, this coincides with the events of Acts 9: 23-25: **"And after that many days were fulfilled, the Jews took counsel to kill him: But their laying await was known of Saul. And they watched the gates day and night to kill him. Then the disciples took him by night, and let him down by the wall in a basket."**

When he leaves the desert, he comes back to Damascus. **"Neither went I up to Jerusalem to them which were apostles before me; but I went into Arabia, and returned again unto Damascus."** Galatians 1:17.

Soon after he arrived in Damascus, he goes Jerusalem. **"Then after three years I went up to Jerusalem to see Peter, and abode with him fifteen days."** Galatians 1:18.

Following the events in Acts, we see this in Acts 9: 26-29: **"And when Saul was come to Jerusalem, he assayed to join himself to the disciples: but they were all afraid of him, and believed not that he was a disciple. But Barnabas took him, and brought him to the apostles, and declared unto them how he had seen the Lord in the way, and that he had spoken to him, and how he had preached boldly at Damascus in the name of Jesus. And he was with them coming in and going out at Jerusalem. And he** spake boldly in the name of the Lord Jesus, and disputed against the Grecians: but they went about to slay him."**

Fearing for his life, he is led of the Lord to leave Jerusalem and go to Carsarea and on to Tarsus. **"Which when the brethren knew, they brought him down to Caesarea, and sent him forth to Tarsus."**

Barnabus goes to meet Paul. **"Then departed Barnabas to Tarsus, for to seek Saul:"** Acts 11: 25.

The two then leave Tarsus and go to Antioch. **"And when he had found him, he brought him unto Antioch. And it came to pass, that a whole year they assembled themselves with the church, and taught much people. And the disciples were called Christians first in Antioch."** Acts 11: 26.

In Antioch they take up an offering for the Disciples being persecuted in Jerusalem and depart for the city to deliver the money collected in their behalf. **"Then the disciples, every man according to his ability, determined to send relief unto the brethren which dwelt in Judaea: Which also they did, and sent it to the elders by the hands of Barnabas and Saul."** Acts 11: 29-30.

Paul tells the story of his conversion a couple of times in the Book of Acts. **And Barnabas and Saul returned from Jerusalem, when they had fulfilled [their] ministry, and took with them John, whose surname was Mark."** Acts 12: 25.

In Acts 22 we are apprised of the reason they leave Jerusalem and go back to Antioch. **"And it came to pass, that, when I was come again to Jerusalem, even while I prayed in** the temple, I was in a trance; And saw him saying unto me, Make haste, and get thee quickly out of Jerusalem: for they will not receive thy testimony concerning me. And I said, Lord, they know that I imprisoned and beat in every synagogue them that believed on thee: And when the blood of thy martyr Stephen was shed, I also was standing by, and consenting unto his death, and kept the raiment of them that slew him. And he said unto me, Depart: for I will send thee far hence unto the Gentiles." Acts 22: 17-21.

In Acts 13 we find his ministry taking a significant step forward. Acts 13: 1-4:

1 Now there were in the church that was at Antioch certain prophets and teachers; as Barnabas, and Simeon that was called Niger, and Lucius of Cyrene, and Manaen, which had been brought up with Herod the tetrarch, and Saul.
2 As they ministered to the Lord, and fasted, the Holy Ghost said, Separate me Barnabas and Saul for the work whereunto I have called them.
3 And when they had fasted and prayed, and laid their hands on them, they sent them away.
4 So they, being sent forth by the Holy Ghost, departed unto Seleucia; and from thence they sailed to Cyprus.

Paul begins preaching what is labeled The Gospel of Christ. **"For I am not ashamed of the gospel of Christ: for it is the power of God unto salvation to every one that believeth; to the Jew first, and also to the Greek."** Romans 1:16.

Does Paul quit saying that Jesus is the Son of God? Most definitely not. But he begins to say that the Son of God died for all mankind. The Gospel of Christ is the death, burial and resurrection of Christ *for the remission of sins*, which you can clearly see in 1 Corinthians 15: 1-4:

> 1 **Moreover, brethren, I declare unto you the gospel which I preached unto you, which also ye have received, and wherein ye stand;**
> 2 **By which also ye are saved, if ye keep in memory what I preached unto you, unless ye have believed in vain.**
> 3 **For I delivered unto you first of all that which I also received, how that Christ died for our sins according to the scriptures;**
> 4 **And that he was buried, and that he rose again the third day according to the scriptures:**

You cannot preach the Gospel of Christ without preaching the Gospel of God, but you can preach the Gospel of God without preaching the Gospel of Christ. What do I mean by that statement? There are some who will tell you that Jesus was the Son of God without saying that He is the only way you can have remission and blotting out of sins.

There are those who say you must be water baptized for remission of sins, and then they quote Acts 2: 38: "**Then Peter said unto them, Repent, and be baptized every one of you in the name of Jesus Christ for the remission of sins, and ye shall receive the gift of the Holy Ghost.**" In other words, there are those that still believe you must do a work before you can be saved. And since baptism is a work they practice that belief.

Many followers of Acts 2: 38 will tell you one cannot be saved apart from water baptism. They err. They prostitute the grace of God. "**For by grace are ye saved through faith;**

and that not of yourselves: it is the gift of God: Not of works, lest any man should boast." Ephesians 2: 8-9.

So, Paul preaches the Gospel of God plus starts adding the Son of God died for our sins. How was the Gospel of Christ revealed? It was revealed to Paul from Old Testament Scripture and is manifest now, by the prophets, for the purpose of obedience.

For I delivered unto you first of all that which I also received, how that Christ died for our sins <u>according to the scriptures</u>; And that he was buried, and that he rose again the third day <u>according to the scriptures</u>: 1 Corinthians 15: 3-4.

Even though the Gospel of Christ was in the Scriptures, it had been kept secret since the world began. Look at Romans 16: 25-26:

> 25 **Now to him that is of power to stablish you according to my gospel, and the preaching of Jesus Christ, according to the revelation of the mystery, which was kept secret since the world began,**
> 26 **But now is made manifest, and by the scriptures of the prophets, according to the commandment of the everlasting God, made known to all nations for the obedience of faith:**

The mystery in the passages above is not the mystery of the Dispensation of the Grace of God that you will find in Ephesians 3: 9: **"And to make all men see what is the fellowship of the mystery, which from the beginning of the world hath been <u>hid in God</u>, who created all things by Jesus Christ:"** The mystery in this passage was one hid in God and not in Scripture.

The mystery hid in Scripture concerns the death, burial and resurrection of Christ for the remission of sins. 1 Corinthians 2: 1-2, Paul states that he came to simply preach Christ crucified.

"And I, brethren, when I came to you, came not with excellency of speech or of wisdom, declaring unto you the testimony of God. For I determined not to know any thing among you, save Jesus Christ, and him crucified."

Why do you suppose God chose to hide this fact? Because if Satan had know that Christ death would be to the saving of the world from death, he would not have been instrumental in Christ's crucifixion. Look at 1 Corinthians 2: 6-8.

> **6 Howbeit we speak wisdom among them that are perfect: yet not the wisdom of this world, nor of the princes of this world, that come to nought:**
> **7 But we speak the wisdom of God in a mystery, even the hidden wisdom, which God ordained before the world unto our glory:**
> **8 Which none of the princes of this world knew: for had they known it, they would not have crucified the Lord of glory.**

It was God's plan for Jesus to be crucified so that He could destroy Satan, who has the power over death. **"Forasmuch then as the children are partakers of flesh and blood, he also himself likewise took part of the same; that through death he might destroy him that had the power of death, that is, the devil; And deliver them who through fear of death were all their lifetime subject to bondage."** Hebrews 2: 14-15.

The ministry of Paul on his first missionary journey is preaching Jesus Christ, and Him crucified for the sins of the world. Even though that message can be found in the Scripture, it was not understood until God revealed it to Paul.

So, Jesus was turned over to the Devil to deliver the world from bondage. From 9: 00 am to 3: 00 pm God allowed Satan to have the fate of Jesus in his hands, and our Lord was crucified for the sins of the world, thus confirming the New Testament.

Hebrews 9: 16-18; 25-26:

> **16** For where a testament is, there must also of necessity be the death of the testator.
> **17** For a testament is of force after men are dead: otherwise it is of no strength at all while the testator liveth.
> **18** Whereupon neither the first [testament] was dedicated without blood.
>
> **25** Nor yet that he should offer himself often, as the high priest entereth into the holy place every year with blood of others;
> **26** For then must he often have suffered since the foundation of the world: but now once in the end of the world hath he appeared to put away sin by the sacrifice of himself.

When Jesus was crucified, the Old Testament law was terminated. Hebrews 10: 9-14:

> **9** Then said he, Lo, I come to do thy will, O God. He taketh away the first, that he may establish the second.

10 By the which will we are sanctified through the offering of the body of Jesus Christ once for all.
11 And every priest standeth daily ministering and offering oftentimes the same sacrifices, which can never take away sins: But this man, after he had offered one sacrifice for sins for ever, sat down on the right hand of God;
12 But this man, after he had offered one sacrifice for sins for ever, sat down on the right hand of God;
13 From henceforth expecting till his enemies be made his footstool. For by one offering he hath perfected for ever them that are sanctified.
14 For by one offering he hath perfected for ever them that are sanctified.

With Jesus' death, the Old Covenant God made with Israel was taken away in order that a New Covenant could be established – with Israel. It has not been established yet for Israel, for they have been set aside, become Lo-Ammi.

But let us get back to the discussion of Paul's ministry. Paul wrote thirteen books: Romans through Philemon. Since we are tracing Paul's ministry in the Book of Acts, you should know that Romans, 1 Corinthians, 2 Corinthians, Galatians, 1 Thessalonians and 2 Thessalonians were written during Acts 18, 19 and 20.

A little earlier in this book, we stated that In Romans 11: 11-18:

1. The olive tree represented the religious privileges of Israel but not Israel perse.
2. That unbelieving Israel is the broken branch.

3. A Gentile who fear God and did works of righteousness could be grafted in.
4. The hope of Israel was extended to the Gentiles.

You need to understand that the Gospel of Christ is to the Jew first until Acts Chapter 20.

Romans 3: 1-2: **"What advantage then hath the Jew? or what profit is there of circumcision? Much every way: chiefly, because that unto them were committed the oracles of God."**

Be very clear, the Jew HAD the advantage at one point in time and circumcision was profitable, especially for the Gentile who, by the act of circumcision became Jewish proselytes. Salvation, in the beginning, was to the Jew first and those Gentiles who feared God.

Acts 13: 16: **"Then Paul stood up, and beckoning with his hand said, Men of Israel, and ye that fear God, give audience."**

Acts 13: 26: **"Men and brethren, children of the stock of Abraham, and whosoever among you feareth God, to you is the word of this salvation sent."**

That is what Paul preached in his early ministry. The Gentiles that were being saved during this time period were partakers of the promises given to the Jews. Look at his teaching as recorded in Galatians 4: 28: **"Now we, brethren, as Isaac was, are the children of promise."**

In Ephesians 2: 11-12 there are Gentile believers who were aliens from the commonwealth of Israel and strangers from the covenants of promise. If we use deductive reasoning, we can say that the saved Gentiles in the churches of Rome, Corinth, Galatia, Thessalonica and some in Ephesus were in the covenants of promise.

In Acts 20: 19-21 we read: **"Serving the Lord with all humility of mind, and with many tears, and temptations, which befell me by the lying in wait of the Jews: And how I kept back nothing that was profitable unto you, but have shewed you, and have taught you publickly, and from house to house, Testifying both to the Jews, and also to the Greeks, repentance toward God, and faith toward our Lord Jesus Christ."**

If you look at verses carefully, you will notice that repentance is toward God and not Jesus Christ.

Later on there were saved Gentiles who were not partakers of the promises of Israel. These are the ones Ephesians 2: 12 addresses. **"That at that time ye were without Christ, being aliens from the commonwealth of Israel, and strangers from the covenants of promise, having no hope, and without God in the world:"**

These Gentiles had no hope of salvation, but something happened to change that. Look at Ephesians 2: 13: **"But now in Christ Jesus ye who sometimes were far off are made nigh by the blood of Christ."**

So we can summarize that there were two groups of believers in the church at Ephesians, those who first trusted and those who also trusted later on. **"That we should be to the praise of his glory, who first trusted in Christ. In whom ye also trusted, after that ye heard the word of truth, the gospel of your salvation: in whom also after that ye believed, ye were sealed with that holy Spirit of promise,"** Ephesians 1:

12-13. These two verses compare favorably with Ephesians 2: 12-18.

The Gentiles of time past were partakers of the covenants of promise and the Gentiles of the "now" times were not. Why? Because Paul has been given a further revelation from God and he starts preaching the Gospel of the Grace of God. Acts 20: 24: "**But none of these things move me, neither count I my life dear unto myself, so that I might finish my course with joy, and the ministry, which I have received of the Lord Jesus, to testify the gospel of the grace of God.**"

The Gospel of the Grace of God is the Gospel of Christ but according to the foundation laid by Paul. A foundation that he started building in his early ministry, but was not consummated until God revealed to him the missing pieces.

In 1 Corinthians 3: 10-11, we read: "**According to the grace of God which is given unto me, as a wise masterbuilder, I have laid the foundation, and another buildeth thereon. But let every man take heed how he buildeth thereupon. For other foundation can no man lay than that is laid, which is Jesus Christ.**"

Now look at Ephesians 2: 20: "**And are built upon the foundation of the apostles and prophets, Jesus Christ himself being the chief corner stone;**"

What we have here is Paul acknowledging that he is preaching Christ is the foundation, just as the apostles and prophets before him were doing, but he cautions those to take heed how one builds upon that foundation. The foundation that Paul built on Christ was a foundation for the temple, which is the Body of Christ.

1 Corinthians 6: 19: "**What? know ye not that your body is the temple of the Holy Ghost which is in you, which ye have of God, and ye are not your own?**"

That foundation built on Christ for the Body of Christ involved an order of Christ's resurrection. 2 Timothy 2: 7-8. "**Consider what I say; and the Lord give thee understanding in all things. Remember that Jesus Christ of the seed of David was <u>raised from the dead according to my gospel:</u>**"

Peter also preached Christ as the foundation, but Peter's foundation had Christ being resurrected to return to Earth and reign for 1,000 years. Did Paul preach that? No, he did not. Paul's preaching of Christ's resurrection was all about Christ seated at the right hand of the father, far above all heavens.

Ephesians 4: 10: "**He that descended is the same also that ascended up far above all heavens, that he might fill all things.)**"

Ephesians 1: 20: "**Which he wrought in Christ, when he raised him from the dead, and set him at his own right hand in the heavenly places,**"

That is why he wrote that followers of his gospel ought to set their minds on heavenly things and not earthly things. Colossians 3: 1-4:

> 1 **If ye then be risen with Christ, seek those things which are above, where Christ sitteth on the right hand of God.**
> 2 **Set your affection on things above, not on things on the earth.**

> 3 For ye are dead, and your life is hid with Christ in God.
> 4 When Christ, who is our life, shall appear, then shall ye also appear with him in glory.

So, I know that Peter's preaching of Christ and His resurrection are not the same as Paul's preaching of Christ and His resurrection. If that is true, and it is, then I also know Peter did not lay the same foundation that Paul did.

Peter and the twelve were laying a foundation for the restoration of Israel to the land of promise, as is seen by their question in Acts 1:6: **"When they therefore were come together, they asked of him, saying, Lord, wilt thou at this time restore again the kingdom to Israel?"**

It is no wonder that the Lord did not answer that question directly, for He who knows all things, knew that God would raise up Paul before Israel was restored. Acts 1: 7-8: **"And he said unto them, It is not for you to know the times or the seasons, which the Father hath put in his own power. But ye shall receive power, after that the Holy Ghost is come upon you: and ye shall be witnesses unto me both in Jerusalem, and in all Judaea, and in Samaria, and unto the uttermost part of the earth."**

* The Gospel of the Grace of God is the good news that Christ died for ALL men. 1 Timothy 2: 1-6:

> 1 I exhort therefore, that, first of all, supplications, prayers, intercessions, and giving of thanks, be made for all men;
> 2 For kings, and for all that are in authority; that we may lead a quiet and peaceable life in all godliness and honesty.

3 For this is good and acceptable in the sight of God our Saviour;
4 Who will have all men to be saved, and to come unto the knowledge of the truth.
5 For there is one God, and one mediator between God and men, the man Christ Jesus;
6 Who gave himself a ransom for all, to be testified in due time.

Titus 2: 11-14:

11 For the grace of God that bringeth salvation hath appeared to all men,
12 Teaching us that, denying ungodliness and worldly lusts, we should live soberly, righteously, and godly, in this present world;
13 Looking for that blessed hope, and the glorious appearing of the great God and our Saviour Jesus Christ;
14 Who gave himself for us, that he might redeem us from all iniquity, and purify unto himself a peculiar people, zealous of good works.

Titus 3: 4-7:

4 But after that the kindness and love of God our Saviour toward man appeared,
5 Not by works of righteousness which we have done, but according to his mercy he saved us, by the washing of regeneration, and renewing of the Holy Ghost;
6 Which he shed on us abundantly through Jesus Christ our Saviour;
7 That being justified by his grace, we should be made heirs according to the hope of eternal life.

* The Gospel of the Grace of God does not put restrictions on anyone. When the Gospel of the Grace of God began to be taught by Paul, Gentiles did not have to bless Israel, keep the law, or refrain from observing ordinances or things offensive to the Jew, as we saw in Acts 15: 19-21:

> **19 Wherefore my sentence is, that we trouble not them, which from among the Gentiles are turned to God:**
> **20 But that we write unto them, that they abstain from pollutions of idols, and from fornication, and from things strangled, and from blood.**
> **21 For Moses of old time hath in every city them that preach him, being read in the synagogues every sabbath day.**

The middle wall of partition has been broken down, (Ephesians 2: 14-15: **"For he is our peace, who hath made both one, and hath broken down the middle wall of partition between us; Having abolished in his flesh the enmity, even the law of commandments contained in ordinances; for to make in himself of twain one new man, so making peace;"**) and the two groups of Gentiles are now one in the Lord.

There are those who teach that the two being made one are Jew and Gentile, but I think the evidence presented here shows otherwise. You must search the Scriptures yourself to verify that. I believe the two groups to be Gentiles who either kept certain ordinances or did not keep those ordinances. This was accomplished *by* what happen on the cross, and not necessarily *at* the time of the cross.

Final Conclusion:

1. The Church the Body of Christ could not have begun at Acts 2 because Paul said he laid the foundation for it and Paul is not saved until Acts 9.
   a. An integral part of this foundation concerns a resurrection in heavenly places. 2 Timothy 2: 7: **"Remember that Jesus Christ of the seed of David was raised from the dead according to my gospel:"**
   b. Peter preached Christ resurrected to sit on an earthly throne.
2. The Church the Body of Christ could not have begun at Acts 28 because Paul was laying the foundation before that, as is evident in 1 Corinthians 12: 13: **"For by one Spirit are we all baptized into one body, whether we be Jews or Gentiles, whether we be bond or free; and have been all made to drink into one Spirit."**
3. The Gospel of the Grace of God is mentioned in Acts 20 and in Acts 28, Israel became Lo-Ammi.
4. True, there were some Gentiles being saved and becoming a part of the Body of Christ having blessed Israel, but they were part of that which was built upon the foundation laid by Paul. Ephesians 2: 20 **"And are built upon the foundation of the apostles and prophets, Jesus Christ himself being the chief corner stone;"**
5. So, we conclude that the Body of Christ had to begin with Paul immediately after he was saved in Acts 9.
6. With the breaking down of the Middle Wall of Partition also came the dissolving of ordinances imposed on the Gentiles who first believed. When that happened, the Gentiles who were not partakers of the promise and those who first believed became one unified body.

God's Time Chart

From the beginning, God had a plan for mankind. The Time Chart is my interpretation, graphically, of that plan. The unfolding of that plan was designed and orchestrated by God, but it is the responsibility of all Christians to study and know it. Our ultimate goal should be to learn more about God. It is my hope that this chart will help you in your pursuit to reach that goal.

This chart is color coded to make it easier to identify specific areas of Biblical transition.

1. Red: Represents the age of the Mystery and the Dispensation of Grace, and The Church the Body of Christ.
2. Blue: Represents Israel and Prophecy and the Dispensation of the Law.
3. Orange: Represent things concerning Satan.
4. Purple: Represents the Throne of God and the heaven above all heavens.

Even though the whole Bible is **FOR** us, not all of the Bible is **TO** us. The Bible must be **"Rightly Divided"** if you are going to understand it fully. Read (2 Timothy 2: 15)

Let us begin to understand the chart.

In the Old Testament:
- Before God created Adam & Eve he created angels. Lucifer, one of them, led a rebellion and was cast out of heaven to earth. After many years he succeeds in destroying God's perfect creation. God flooded the earth and re-created it. Genesis 1:2 forward is the re-creation and the heaven (firmament) in vs. 6-8 is the home of Satan today.
- God established a perfect place for Adam and gave him dominion. (Genesis 1: 26-28)

- But sin entered in and God pronounced a curse on mankind. (Gen. 3:14-19)
- Later, God told Abraham he would be a blessing and He would make of him a great nation, (Gen. 12:1-3) and then entered into an everlasting Covenant to be his God. (Gen. 17:6-8)
- God promised that Jesus would come as a king (Isa. 9:6, 7; Dan. 7:9-14; Zech. 14:9) and would reign in Jerusalem (Isa. 2:1-5; Ezek. 11:14-21).
- Israel, as a nation, rejected Jesus as the Messiah (Savior), so God foretells of her destruction and dispersion. (Isa. 6:9-12)

In the four Gospels:
- We are told of the earthly ministry of Christ, His birth (Luke 1:31-33)
- His Message (Matt. 4:17)
- His instructions to the twelve disciples (John 18:36, 37)
- His betrayal by Judas (Luke 22:3-6)
- His resurrection (Luke 24:1-6)

The Son of God came to Earth but the world did not know Him as the Son of God or the Savior of the world. (John 1:10) His own people, the Jews, did not accept him as Messiah (John 1:11), they rejected Him.

The Acts period has often been referred to as the book between. It is in this book that the fall of Isreal is chronicled.
- Peter presents the message of the kingdom. (Acts 2:29-38)
- Some believed it and some did not. (Acts 28:24)
- Since the Jewish nation as a whole did not believe Messiah had come to establish His kingdom, God blinded the Jew. (Acts 28:25-28)
- But Acts also marks the beginning of the Church the Body of Christ with the salvation of Paul in Chapter 9.

The Pauline Epistles are Romans-Philemon and reveal the special ministry of Paul and subsequent Dispensation of Grace.
- The revelation of the Mystery: hid in Scripture (Rom. 16:25,26; and hid in God (Eph. 3:1-5; Col. 1: 25-27)
- The Dispensation Of Grace: (Eph. 3:2)
- The mystery of the Church the Body of Christ (Rom, 12:5; 1 Cor. 10:17; 12:27; Eph. 1:22,23; 2:14-15; 3:6; 4:4; Col. 1:18; 3:25)
- The Gospel of the Grace of God: (Rom. 3:24; 1 Cor. 15:1-4; Eph. 2:8,9; Titus 3:7)
  This gospel is about:
  1. The preaching of the cross as salvation for mankind. (1 Cor. 1:17,18; Gal. 6:14; Col. 1:20)
  2. Forgiveness of sin by the blood of Christ (Rom. 3:25; 5:9; Eph. 1:7; Col. 1:14)
  3. One baptism (Eph. 4:5)
  4. And a greater commission than that given to the twelve disciples (2 Cor. 5:14-20)
  5. A heavenly kingdom in deference to an earthly kingdom (Eph. 1:3; 2:6; Phil. 3:20; Col. 3:1-3)

The prophesied message of an earthly kingdom for the Jew is in abeyance until the rapture of the Church the Body of Christ. (1 Cor. 15: 51-52; Phil. 3:20, 21; Col. 3:4; 1 Thess. 4:13-18)

The Book of Revelation chronicles the 7 years of tribulation and the millennial reign of Christ. He will defeat the Devil at the end of the 1000 year reign and establish the long awaited Kingdom on earth, which will be the new heaven and new earth.

"Time Past" is all about Israel; **"But Now"** is all about Gentiles in the Dispensation of Grace, and **"Restitution & Refreshing"** is the promise to restore Isreal coming to fruition.

Eternity Future is a segregated place.

1. The Church the Body of Christ is far above all heavens.
2. The faithful 12 tribes of the Jews will be in the New Jerusalem.
3. All others will be living on earth.

The Limited Knowledge Series Volume One

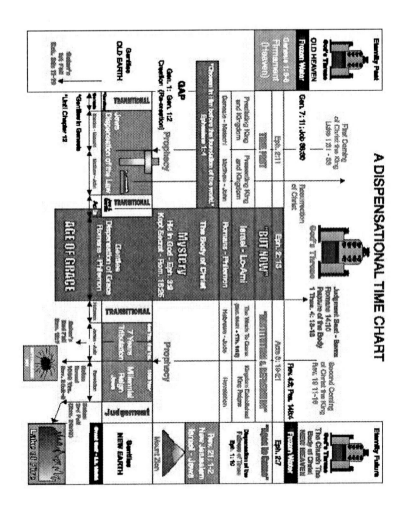